Patterns 2
Interactions and building blocks

Schools Council Integrated Science Project

The Schools Council Integrated Science Project was set up at Chelsea College, London, from 1969 to 1975. The project team have developed their materials in association with many teachers and have tested them in a wide range of schools.

Organisers
W. C. Hall
B. S. Mowl

Team members
J. I. Bausor
Mrs M. P. Jarman
Miss B. A. Lawes
M. R. Nice
D. Wimpenny

Northern Ireland coordinator
S. J. McGuffin

Patterns 2
Interactions and building blocks

Authors
William Hall
Brian Mowl
John Bausor

Contributor
Michael Bradshaw

Published for
the Schools Council
by Longman

LONGMAN GROUP LIMITED, London
for the Schools Council

© Schools Council Publications 1973

First published 1973
Second impression 1975
ISBN 0 582 34010 1

Phototypeset by Oliver Burridge Filmsetting Limited, Crawley
Printed in Great Britain by Compton Printing Limited

Contents

v

Acknowledgements

We are grateful to the following for permission to reproduce copyright material: The Anti-Concorde Project for The Anti-Concorde advertisement as appeared in *The Times*, 18 May 1970; Collins Publishers for extracts from *Pesticides and Pollution* by Dr Kenneth Mellanby; David & Charles (Holdings) Ltd., for an extract from *The Elements Rage* by Frank W. Lane; General Accident Fire and Life Assurance Corporation Ltd. for an extract from their Home Policy; *The Guardian* for the following articles, 'Waste Plastic could be used as fuel' from *The Guardian*, 22 May 1970, and an article on hurricanes; Ian Breach for 'The Criminal Classes' from *The Guardian*, 8 May 1972; the author for his letter to *The Times*, 1 June 1971 entitled 'Pollution Growth' by Ivor H. Mills; IPC Transport Press Ltd. for an article 'Not Criminal' from *Motor*, 17 May 1972; *The Sun* for an article 'Doomwatch menace – Top Scientist warns of the Plastic Peril' from *The Sun*, 15 April 1970 and Syndication International for the article 'End of D.D.T. Decade' from *Science Journal*, January 1970.

The authors and publisher are grateful to the following for permission to reproduce photographs: Aerofilms, page 94 top left and right; ARC Weed Research organization, page 6 right; Australian News and Information Bureau, page 14; B and R Relays, page 47 right; Barnaby's Picture Library, pages 78 centre left and 100; Black and Decker Ltd, page 40 bottom left; British Domestic Appliances Ltd, page 40 left centre and bottom right; British Leyland UK Ltd, page 102; British Museum (Natural History), page 13 centre and right; British Airways, page 53 bottom; British Rail, pages 104 and 115; British Steel Corporation, page 53 centre; British Waterways Board, page 119 top; Burts and Harvey Ltd, page 10 left; Eric Buston and Associates Ltd, page 80 top right; J. Allen Cash, page 129 left; CERN, page 97 left; Civic Trust, page 132 left; John Clegg, pages 3 and 12 left; Cotton, Silk and Man-made Fibres Research Association, page 31; Dr H E Egerton, page 110; Electrolux, page 40 top left; English Electric Co Ltd, page 66 top; Forestry Commission, page 78 bottom right; Foster Transformers Ltd, page 66 centre; Fox Photos Ltd, page 36 bottom; GPO, pages 71 centre and 74 bottom; Crown © Geological Survey photographs reproduced by permission of the Controller, HMSO, pages 76, 77, 79, 84 except centre left, 85, 93 right, 95 and 96; Goodmans Loudspeakers Ltd, page 68 top left; GLC, page 36 top; James Hall (Photographers) Ltd, page 106; Philip Harris Ltd, page 109 top right; Hydrocut Ltd, page 10 right; IBM United Kingdom Ltd, pages 72 left and 73; ICI Fibres Ltd, pages 28–9 and 34; Industrial Diamond Co Ltd, page 146 left; Industrial Magnets Ltd, page 47 left; ITT Creed, page 71 top; A. F. Kersting, pages 131 left and 132 right; Keystone Press Agency Ltd, pages 42 bottom and 92; John Lawrence, page 72 right; London Stone Cleaning and Restoration Co, 80 top left; Catherine Matthews, page 80 bottom left; R. O. Muir, pages 84 centre left and 93 left; National Coal Board, pages 83 and 146 right; National Farmers' Union, page 78 top; Natural History Photographic Agency, page 12 right; Novosti Press Agency, page 119 bottom; Ordnance Survey, Crown ©, pages 152 and 153 Pace, page 42 top; John Player and Sons Motorsport Agency, page 97 top right; Plessey Telecommunications Ltd, pages 68 bottom and 69; Paul Popper, pages 80 bottom right and 159; Rank Xerox Ltd, page 74 top; Royal Astronomical Society, photo from Mt. Wilson and Palomar Observatories, page 142; The Royal Institution, pages 60 and 64; Shell Photographic Service, page 97 bottom right; Edwin Smith, page 131 right; Spalding Bulb Co Ltd, page 78 bottom left; Standard Telephones and Cables Ltd, pages 67 and 68 top right; Syndication International, page 87; Thorn Domestic Appliances (Electrical) Ltd, pages 40 top right and 101; Wellcome Museum of Medical Science, page 13 left.

Foreword

This *Pupils' manual* is one of a series designed to provide a scheme of work in science. This scheme is divided into three parts:

Part 1   Building blocks (*Patterns 1* and *2*)
Part 2   Energy (*Patterns 3*)
Part 3   Interactions (*Patterns 4*)

The *Pupils' manuals* are not textbooks containing information for you to memorise. Their purpose is to guide you in experimenting, and in examining other scientists' experiments, and to help you discuss the ways in which science affects people. The *Pupils' manuals* are only a part of the scheme: you will be given other books to read, films to watch and experiments to perform which are different from, or in addition to those which appear in these pages.

In *Patterns 1* you investigated a variety of building blocks ranging from planets to particles. Similar questions were asked of each of the building blocks and some of their relationships were established.

In this book you will first be investigating patterns of interactions between selected building blocks of different sizes. The last two sections are concerned with the classification and distribution of building blocks.

9 Competition and predation

You may know something about the life and habits of the robin. It lives in gardens and parks, indeed almost anywhere with bushes and trees to provide cover. In spring and summer a pair of robins occupy a definite area of ground called their territory: this is their habitat. During the breeding season the robins will spend all their time in the territory, feeding and raising their family. The robins resolutely and fiercely defend their territory against others from neighbouring areas and there are often struggles and chases. It is difficult to imagine a more unsuitable tribute to the season of peace and goodwill than portraying this aggressive little bird on Christmas cards! Nevertheless, what aspects of its life illustrate the twin themes of the section? In what interactions is the robin involved? What is the outcome of the territorial behaviour of the robins? In this section you will be searching for patterns which may answer questions similar to these.

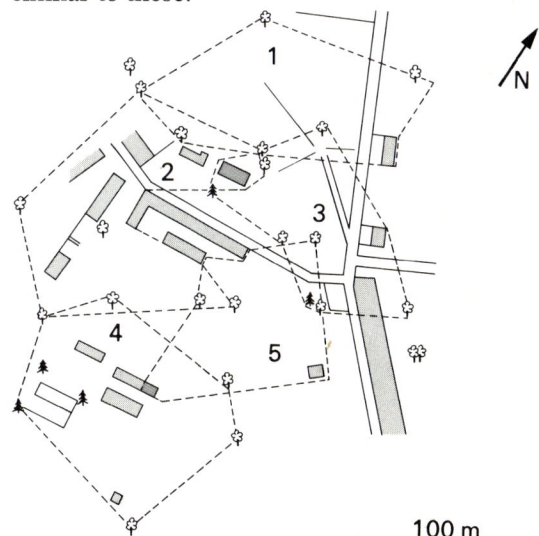

Figure 9.1
The territories of five robins. They have been mapped by careful observation of the birds (shading shows where territories overlap)

100 m

Investigation 9.1 Growing populations together

In *Patterns 1*, Section 3 populations of two similar organisms, *Tribolium confusum* and *Tribolium castaneum*, were placed together to investigate the effects that this might have on the population growth of each type. Figure 9.2 shows the growth of populations of *Tribolium*. How does it compare with populations of two different types grown together?

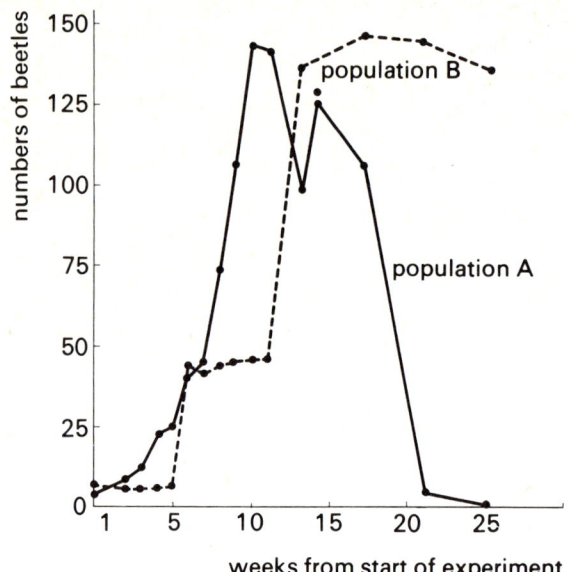

Figure 9.2
Changes in size of two populations of *Tribolium* beetles

You have used the small floating plant called *Lemna* before. Figure 9.3 shows the growth of populations of two types of *Lemna* both together and separately. Are there any similarities with the *Tribolium* populations?

	number of animals in 0.5 cm^3			
	population size when grown separately		population size when grown together	
days	*P. caudatum*	*P. aurelia*	*P. caudatum*	*P. aurelia*
2	47	29	19	30
4	85	182	25	141
6	122	322	—	220
8	131	399	21	163
10	166	455	13	176
12	146	489	15	278
14	111	468	12	221
16	139	478	0	220

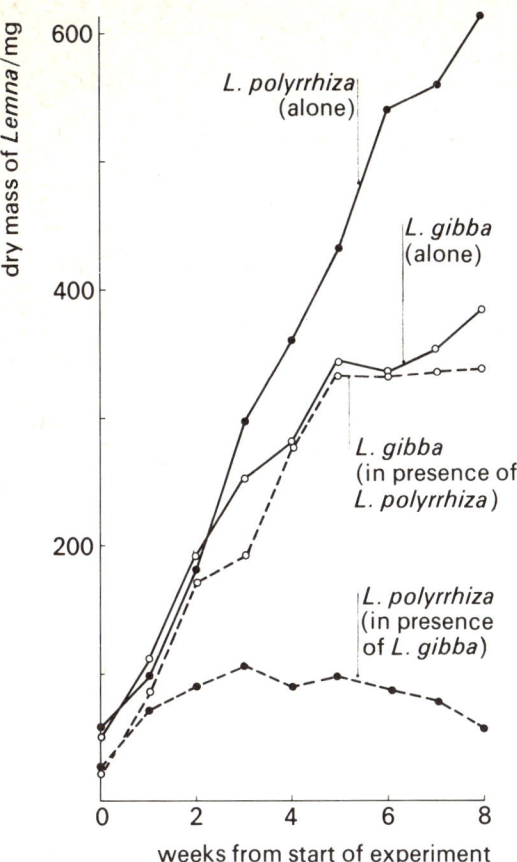

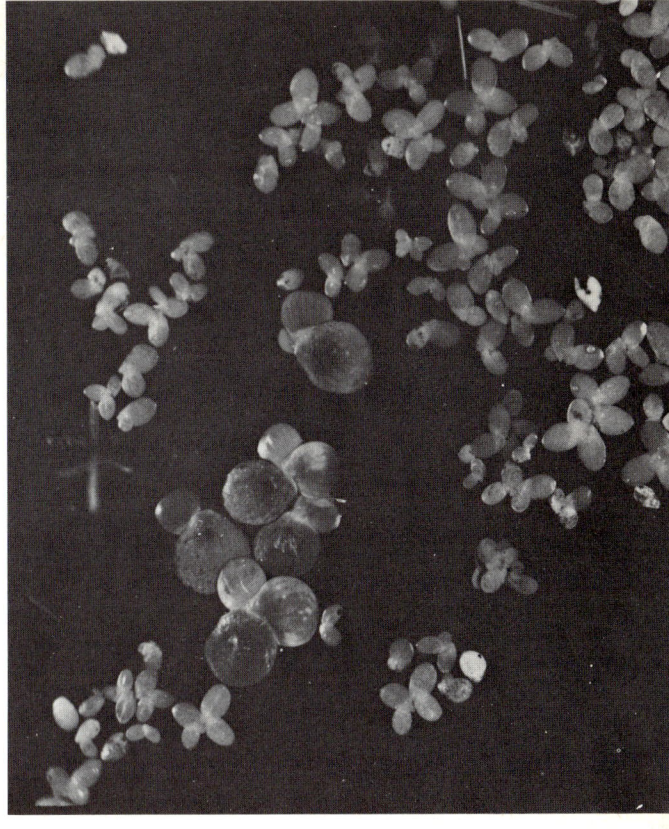

Figure 9.3
The growth of population of *Lemna gibba* and *Lemna polyrrhiza* separately and together. All populations were grown under identical conditions

Figure 9.4
Lemna minor and *Lemna polyrrhiza* floating together on the water surface. Are they present in your mini-pond communities? If not keep a watch for them. How might they affect each other if present in the same mini-pond?

The tables on page 2 gives the results of an investigation into the population growth of two types of *Paramecium*, an animal with which you are probably familiar. Neither feeds on the other and populations were kept, as far as possible, under identical conditions.

What is the purpose of growing the populations of the types of *Paramecium* separately?

There will also be a demonstration for you to examine. This is an investigation into growing a crop plant and a weed together.

Do the experiments and other information show a pattern? If

populations of organisms compete what resources are they competing for?

All of the investigations which have been performed or described concern two populations in a laboratory. Do you think they are realistic 'models' of what might actually happen in a community?

Investigation 9.2 Investigating population growth patterns

You will need

Part a   Results of investigations into population growth
▷ Part b   A population of *Drosophila* (or other organism) which has reached the upper limit of its growth

Part a

The pattern of population growth is typically one in which the numbers reach an upper limit and then they begin to decline (or they may remain stable or decline and increase in a series of cycles). ▶Explain this pattern of population growth. ◀

▷ Part b

▶Predict the effect on population growth of removing a limiting resource. Devise a way, using the organism(s) available to you, of testing your prediction. ◀

Investigation 9.3 A limit to the growth of the human population?

In a previous investigation you discussed the growth of the human population. So far, at least, this seems to be a typical example of the population growth pattern. But, as you saw, difficulties in forecasting the future size of the human population arise because of the enormous number of other factors which may have an influence on it. For the same reasons it would be wise to be cautious about predicting that the members of the human population will eventually be involved in competitive interactions for limited resources which would result in a nil population growth, or even the decline in size which is typical of other populations.

Not least amongst the reasons for caution is the fact that man himself has some control over possible limiting resources. The supply of a resource such as food would be an example. For any other population this could well be a limiting resource but, because

4

man's technological knowledge can be applied to produce more food, it may not be a limiting resource affecting the growth of his own population. What else might act as a limiting resource on the human population? Is it possible to be sure about your suggestions? Discuss the reasons for the answers you give to these questions.

In the meantime there are some who believe that the effects of competition can be detected in human society even now. The following are extracts from a letter, by a scientist, to a national newspaper (look up any unfamiliar words in a dictionary):

Many of us think that affluence may also place a strain on a society. When affluence and numbers rise together the competition becomes increasingly severe. It is affluence which draws people to the cities and away from the rural areas: they move partly to get more money but partly to get more of the so-called good things of life. It is in the cities that the pressure of numbers and competition for work become most intense.

Such evidence as we have indicates that the cracks which are appearing in the structure of society are most readily seen in the urban areas. It is not surprising that the escalating crimes of violence occur there, because the financial rewards of robbery may be greater, but the abuse of drugs is also more apparent in city life. Frequently the drug-takers make it plain that they indulge in their habits to escape from the strains of life. For some, even that is not enough and they end up taking an overdose of drugs with potential suicidal results. Our most recent studies suggest that attempted suicide in the city of Cambridge is two or three times as pre-

valent as in the surrounding rural areas. Similar data are available for Edinburgh.

That intense competition leads to destruction of animal societies has now been shown by Professor James Henry. He was one of the team which trained the chimpanzees to operate the apparatus in space capsules before man went into space. The chimpanzees all developed high blood pressure. He has now shown that keeping mice in a series of boxes joined by tubes in which they can only just pass each other leads to the emergence of dominant males who have severe hypertension and 'drop-outs' with normal blood pressure who withdraw from society. The hypertensive mice develop heart disease and die of coronary thrombosis. The similarity to human society is striking.

Prospective studies of persons with so-called 'pattern A behaviour' show that those with driving personalities who are always working to dead-lines and striving to get to the top have a very much higher incidence of coronary thrombosis than the 'pattern B' individuals who take life as it comes.

It may not impress people that among women in their twenties 3 per cent will attempt suicide before they reach their thirties, or that in some organisations 20 per cent have had to be treated with anti-depressant drugs. But how long can a society with its present numbers withstand such a disruptive state of affairs? With an even larger population competition would be more intense and it is then doubtful if living would be worth while for anyone.

We urgently need to know what percentage of disturbed people a civilised community can tolerate without progressive disruption of the society. We might even find that the present population is too large when competition intensifies as we are all cajoled to worship the god known as 'increased efficiency'.

Yours faithfully,

IVOR H. MILLS,

Department of Investigative Medicine,
University of Cambridge,
Addenbrooke's Hospital,
Trumpington Street, Cambridge.

What patterns of stress-behaviour and illness does the writer detect as being connected with competition resulting from increasing numbers?

Because the population of the world is growing so fast a great deal of effort is made to improve the yield of crop plants. Since the amount of land is limited, farmers and others concerned have to search for ways of improving food production other than simply by increasing the area of land under cultivation. Much of the rest of this section is concerned with methods by which this may be achieved.

One obvious method to investigate is whether an increased yield would result from sowing more seed in a fixed area of land.

Investigation 9.4 Growing a crop plant at different densities

You will need

plant pots of the same size (about 15–20 cm diameter)
supply of barley seeds
supply of seed compost

▶ Predict and test the effect of increasing the density of seed sown. Discuss and devise ways of finding out if there is an ideal density at which to sow seeds. ◀

Figure 9.5
These seedlings of a cereal plant in a field give some idea of the density at which they are normally grown

Figure 9.6
A crop seriously affected by wildoats.

Since competition takes place between organisms man is especially concerned about his own competitors – organisms such as weeds and pests which compete with him, directly or indirectly, for his own foods. In Great Britain alone the annual loss to the yield of cereal crops caused by weed infestation is somewhere in the region of £50 million. To combat this threat a variety of methods is used.

Those used against weeds include mechanical methods (hoeing is a simple example) and chemical methods (such as the use of herbicides). Despite the undoubted advantages to be gained by eliminating weeds from fields planted with crops and other places, most methods seem to have undesirable side effects which do not often become clear until the method has been in use for some time. What is needed to prevent this happening?

Here are some views on the use of different methods of controlling weeds.

Investigation 9.5 The advantages and disadvantages of different forms of weed control

'Total and permanent destruction of all vegetation is sometimes required, for instance, on railway tracks, on garden paths and around farm buildings. Mechanical methods such as hoeing were the earliest and are still common. Destruction may be better accomplished by burning, either of dead grass on the surface, or more efficiently using a flame gun. Burning can kill germinating seedlings and the parts of plants above the surface, but even with the largest flame gun it is almost impossible for the heat to penetrate deep enough to kill underground seeds . . . that are buried at all deeply. The difficulty of controlling a perennial weed like creeping thistle is easily demonstrated at the site of a bonfire on infested ground. Though such a fire may have burned hotly for days, it is not uncommon to see thistle shoots appear in the middle of a burned area of several square yards within a few weeks. This cannot be due to inward growth from unaffected areas; the rhizomes* immediately under the fire must have survived. Burning and hoeing has the disadvantage that the soil is not rendered "immune" to further weed attack; where crops are to be grown after the weeds are destroyed this is an obvious advantage, but some lasting treatment is desired on other areas.

*Rhizomes – underground parts of the plant from which fresh growth can start.

7

'Herbicides have proved very useful for total weed control. Sodium chlorate . . . is still widely used, sometimes in doses of more than a hundredweight to the acre. . . . No plants will grow for at least six months after a heavy dressing of sodium chlorate, but when it is finally washed away it has no serious after effects. Even in high doses there is remarkably little effect on the soil fauna.★ Borax is also used as a total weedkiller. It is rather more slow-acting than sodium chlorate, and also more persistent. It does not seem to have a great effect on the soil fauna, nor to other forms of wild life.'

but in talking about grass verges along roadsides, the writer states:

'In recent years labour costs have risen, and workers have become scarce. Most farming processes have been mechanised, and so has roadside grass cutting. First ordinary farm mowing machines were used; these could only cut smooth and level areas. More versatile machines have been developed, able to work on rougher ground. The trouble with these is that many areas are too rough even for such tools, and also that this cutting has to be repeated several times in the season. The cost of cutting is considerable, but that of removing the cut vegetation, which is usually necessary, is even greater. The cut vegetation can sometimes be sold as hay, but is usually too weedy and polluted by dust from passing traffic to be worth the cost of collection. If left uncollected the cut material may dry and increase the danger of fire, or in wet weather it may kill underlying plants and produce unsightly dead patches. Mechanical cutting has generally been accepted by conservationists and naturalists, partly perhaps because it is not too efficient and has a minimum effect on the rough areas which the machinery cannot easily reach.

'Many County Surveyors thought that the discovery of selective weedkillers had solved their problem. They wished to retain grass verges on country roads for aesthetic reasons and to prevent erosion, but they wanted to get rid of all tall plants and to prevent scrubby growth. They hoped that herbicides could be applied more cheaply than the vegetation could be cut, and that the effects would be longer-lasting. The first attempts were most unfortunate. DNOC applied in summer turned the verges into disgusting areas of dead and dying plants, the spray more often than not drifted into the hedges and damaged them, and many birds, mammals and insects died leaving their corpses for all to see. This process was not continued on any large scale for long, though selective spraying of patches of particularly "objectionable" weeds has occurred. Then MCPA and 2,4-D were used. These were believed to be non-poisonous to wild life (i.e. birds,

★Fauna – animals.

8

mammals, insects, etc.) and were also considerably less expensive than the more poisonous substances. Applications were again made in summer, when many of the more attractive plants were coming up to flower. The immediate result, though perhaps not quite so hideous as that produced by DNOC, was quite horrifying, for the roadsides were soon covered with the twisted and deformed plants where attractive flowers had been expected. The outcry continued, and such spraying has only been continued in a minority of counties. . . .

'Herbicides on roadside verges have the immediate effects noted above. They also have long-term effects on the constitution of the flora* (and therefore of the fauna dependent upon it). There has been surprisingly little scientific work on this long-term effect, the most important exceptions being some interesting experiments which have continued for some twelve years on Akeman Street in Gloucestershire. The botanical† side of this work has been described carefully but the effects on animals do not yet seem to have been assessed. . . .

'The herbicides used in this work are not highly poisonous, and it is unlikely that many forms of animal life are killed directly by their use. This has encouraged the statement that they are "harmless to wild life", which ignores their effect on plants and on the animal species dependent on affected plants. For this reason most conservationists are still rightly suspicious of this method, and do not wish to see it extended until more research has been done.

'However, we must face the fact that the verges must be prevented from becoming over-grown, and the preferred method of hand cutting is unlikely to be reintroduced, except perhaps in restricted areas of biological importance where voluntary labour may be available. Many authorities are now using flail cutters. These are generally preferred to chemicals by naturalists, though we still know little of the biological effect. Flail cutters reduce the vegetation to a mulch which does little harm and need not be collected. They also kill any animals which get in their way, and although most birds and mammals make their escape, some do not and corpses can usually be found after a machine has passed. Most insects on the vegetation which is cut are also killed; they generally survive hand cutting or ordinary machine mowing. The vegetation of an area regularly cut by the flail method will be different from that resulting from hand cutting, and we do not yet know whether the results will be preferred by naturalists. From their point of view the main advantage over herbicide spraying is that odd corners particularly with rough ground are

*Flora – plants.
†Botanical – botany is the study of plants.

likely to be left by the flail, whereas a spray could easily be squirted wherever the operator wishes; that is to say the flail has the advantage of its comparative inefficiency!'

and in reference to cultivated areas:

'. . . Today it is possible to kill all the grass and most of the other plants by one application of a weedkiller such as Paraquat, and as the herbicide is rapidly rendered inactive by contact with the soil, immediate reseeding is possible. This process needs to be studied carefully, but preliminary observations suggest that it may often be less harmful to the soil fauna than ploughing or other mechanical methods of cultivation. For instance, the surface-casting earthworms, usually almost eliminated by cultivation, may survive. Here again the herbicide, properly used, may be a help and not a danger to conservation.'

(All extracts from Dr Kenneth Mellanby's book *Pesticides and Pollution*, Collins, London, 1967)

As a result of reading these extracts, summarise some of the advantages and disadvantages of the use of mechanical and chemical methods of controlling weeds.

Figure 9.7
a Spraying roadside verges   b Cutting roadside verges

▷ Investigation 9.6 Is using a herbicide more efficient than hoeing or digging?

You will need

any general weedkiller
watering can with a rose attached
a hoe or fork

Choose an area of ground containing similar populations of weeds. Divide into three equal patches. Count the number of weeds in each. (You could go further and count the number of weeds of each type.) Treat each patch as follows.

Patch 1. Apply the weedkiller according to the instructions on the package. It is probably best to do this with a watering can especially kept for applying weedkiller.

Patch 2. Hoe or dig the weeds, removing as much of each plant as you can.

Patch 3. Leave untreated.

When applying weedkiller take care not to let it fall on plants or ground next to the area being treated or splash on yourself or your clothes. Wash your hands thoroughly after using herbicides. Record the weed populations after one week, one month and one term. How do they compare? Which is the most efficient method of weed control? What is the purpose of patch 3? Do the instructions for the weedkiller indicate any disadvantages or advantages of using such preparations connected with the future use of the ground?

Up to this point you have considered only competitive patterns of interaction between organisms, sometimes belonging to the same population, sometimes to different populations. What other patterns of interaction are there?

Investigation 9.7 A further pattern of interaction between populations and organisms

You will need

population of *Hydra* in small glass containers
population of *Daphnia* (water fleas)
other material which you may be given (film loops)
dropper pipette

Place a few *Daphnia* in with the *Hydra*. Describe any interaction you observe.

If possible go outside and look for aphids (greenfly and blackfly) on plants in the school grounds. Roses often support large populations of greenfly and broadbeans are a favourite of blackfly. Make careful observations of the populations. Is there any evidence of an interaction taking place with other organisms? You may be given film loops to watch.

As the result of this investigation, and from your general knowledge, what pattern of interaction can be observed?

Figure 9.8
Hydra is a very small animal (it may be 5 mm tall when fully extended) which spends its life clinging to weeds and stones in ponds

Figure 9.9
A population of aphids

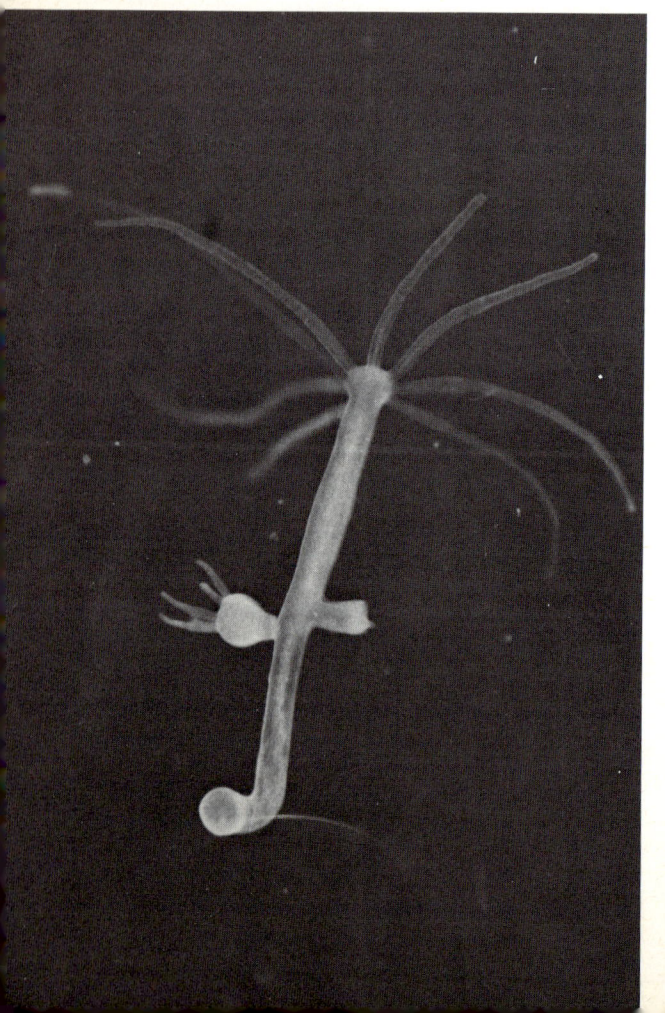

▷ Investigation 9.8 Parasitism – a special sort of predation

Figure 9.10

a The head of a tapeworm. The tapeworm lives in the food canal with its head attached to the walls of the canal. You can see the crown of hooks and large suckers which help it do this

This is mainly a demonstration investigation. You may need a microscope. In what ways are the organisms you study suited to their way of life? How is the pattern of interaction you have examined in this investigation similar to, and different from, those you have studied previously?

b A flea

c A louse

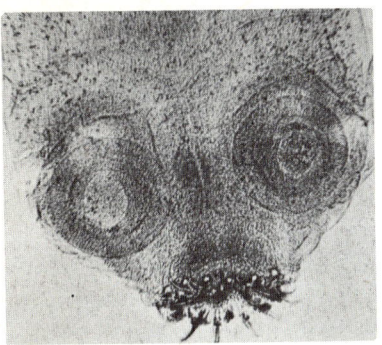

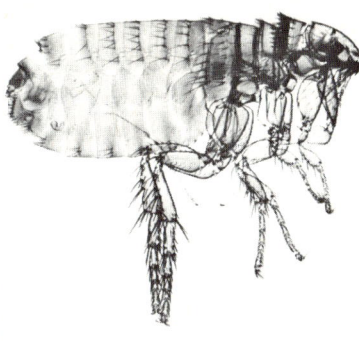

Investigation 9.9 Population interactions and population size

You have already discussed the immediate effects of competition interactions on the size of a population or organisms. ▶Suggest a simple model describing the long-term effect of an interaction between populations of predator (or parasite) and prey (or host) on the size of their populations. Unfortunately to test your suggestion would take far too much time. You will be given some data of tests. Do they support your suggestions?◀

Investigation 9.10 Making use of population interactions – biological control

You will need

film loops *Biological control:* Apanteles *parasite*
            Biological control: Whitefly and Encarsia

In an attempt to regulate or control pests it has often been possible to use their natural predators and parasites. Large numbers of the predator or parasite are reared and then released among the pests. For example, ladybird beetles have been introduced into glass-

Figure 9.11
Biological control of *Opuntia*
(the prickly pear)

houses to feed on aphids which were damaging crop plants. When man makes use of this type of interaction it is called a biological control. The illustrations in figure 9.11 show one success story of biological control.

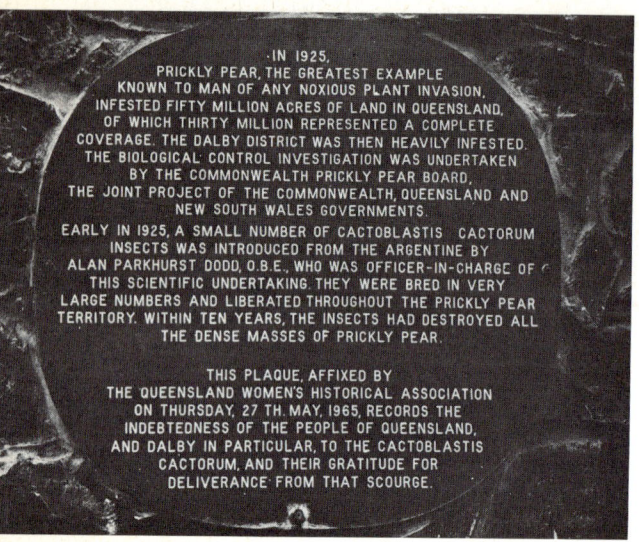

a The plaque tells the story

b An area in Queensland, Australia infested with *Opuntia*

d The same area as in 9.11b showing complete destruction of *Opuntia* by *Cactoblastis* caterpillars

c *Cactoblastis* caterpillars at work

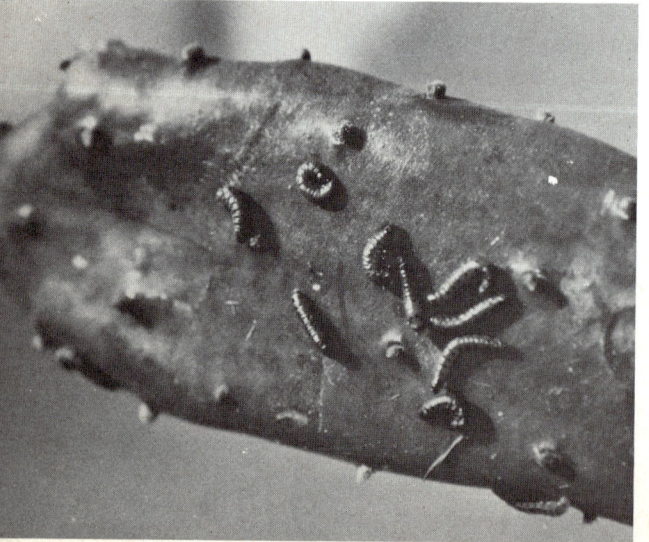

Watch and discuss the film loops.

Attempts at biological control of pests and weeds are not always successful as the two quotations below illustrate. ▶Given the facts explain why you might have predicted the failure of these attempts at biological control. ◀

The house sparrow was introduced from England into the New York district of America. The intention was that it should destroy caterpillars feeding on the leaves of elm trees in the public parks. While the sparrow certainly takes many of the caterpillars it can find, it is not a bird adapted for searching for prey in the foliage of tall trees. Instead of controlling the caterpillars, the sparrow spread beyond New York, began to raid cornfields and became an agricultural pest in many places.

Before myxomatosis arrived, the island of Great Saltee, off the southern coast of Ireland, was overrun by rabbits. In an attempt to control them the owner brought cats to the island and turned them loose, so that they became wild. The cats began to kill some of the birds nesting on the island, which the owner wished to preserve. The number of rabbits did not appear to grow less and, indeed, they extended their range and colonised wider areas than before.

Why should first laboratory tests and then 'field' experiments be carried out on an interaction between a pest and its enemy before the widespread use of the interaction? ▶What is the ideal interaction between pest population and that of the controlling organism? Why could a controlling organism be useless if it totally exterminated the pest in an area? ◀

Investigation 9.11 Further concern over methods of controlling our own competitors

The fact that man is knowingly and unknowingly polluting his planet is a theme considered throughout this course. In many ways the unintentional pollution is by far the most dangerous because it arises out of ignorance – man's ignorance of patterns and consequently his ability to predict the side-effects of his own activities. Discuss what you understand by 'pollution'. In recent years the gradual awareness of the side-effects of the use of pesticides and herbicides have caused widespread concern. In January, 1970, the following appeared in the London magazine *Science Journal* :

End of the DDT decade

There is widespread concern about reports of insecticides found polluting the whole of the globe. They have been found in small amounts in Antarctic penguins, in seals from the Arctic and even in the rain over Britain. We all have small amounts in our tissues. There is no doubt that DDT and other organochlorine insecticides can now be detected by skilful chemists in almost every substance examined. Some scientists have even expressed the view that pesticides are a major risk to the future of mankind.

Only one group of pesticides, the organochlorine insecticides, including DDT, dieldrin, heptachlor and endosulfan, is seriously blamed for this world-wide pollution. Other insecticides may be more acutely poisonous, herbicides carelessly used may have serious ecological* effects on the vegetation, but most of these pesticides soon break down to more or less harmless residues. Organochlorines are only slowly biodegradable,† and some heptachlor, for instance, are turned into more-toxic substances. DDT and dieldrin in soil kills insects ten years after application, . . . and in water in concentrations as low as one part in 10 millions may wipe out fish, insects and crustacea.

In some parts of the world, where pesticides have been grossly overused, serious and probably irreversible ecological results have occurred. In Britain the situation is less serious. In the years before 1962 huge numbers of seed eating birds, particularly pigeons, died from eating corn dressed with dieldrin. Predators, including foxes, badgers, owls and hawks, fed on the poisoned birds and many died. The voluntary ban on dieldrin seed dressing on spring sown corn stopped the mass slaughter. The recently published report for 1966–68 of Monks Wood Experimental Station shows that no permanent damage was done to most species, and that sparrow-hawks and peregrines, which were almost wiped out over large areas of southern Britain, are now making a slow recovery.

Forebodings about the future effects of organochlorine pesticides on the world are based on the assumption that they will be used in ever-increasing quantities. This is, in fact, not happening, for their manufacture is decreasing. In 1968 the United States, the greatest producer (and exporter), made less than half the tonnage produced in 1963; use in Britain, too, shows an annual decrease. DDT is still used very successfully against malaria and other insect-borne diseases in the tropics, saving millions of human lives in a year, and killing pests and so increasing crop yields to feed the millions saved from disease. This will continue but not for long, partly because pest insects are becoming resistant and partly because DDT is being replaced by other, less persistent, chemicals. Organochlorine insecticides were in fact being phased out even before Sweden, Canada and various States in the US banned or severely restricted these chemicals, and this process will undoubtedly continue.

Delegates to the fifth British Insecticide and Fungicide Conference at Brighton in November were shown how the chemical industry is tackling this problem. Sessions dealt specifically with the precautions to safeguard wildlife. Scientists also described many new chemicals, tailor-made to avoid the damage caused by the organochlorines.

Only long and careful ecological investigations will show how safe these new chemicals are, but their study by independent experts before release gives reason to hope that serious damage will be avoided. I therefore do not think that pesticides are likely to be one of the serious causes of world-wide environmental deterioration . . . as it might have done without public vigilance, the global effects could have been appalling. But with their replacement by less ecologically dangerous chemicals, and the ever-increasing research on pest control by cultural and biological methods, there is hope that one danger to our environ-ment may be avoided – providing we continue to be vigilant.

---

* Ecology – the study of plants and animals and their interactions with each other.
† Biodegradable – the property of being broken down by the activity of living things.

Give some examples of organochlorine insecticides. What happens to most insecticides and herbicides? Why are organochlorine insecticides considered to be particularly dangerous? Why can the organochlorines cause the death of animals other than those against which they were originally used? Despite the disadvantages associated with the use of insecticides, what benefits have they brought? Why does the author feel that pesticides will not be a serious cause of world wide pollution? What are the advantages of biological control methods over chemical methods? What are the disadvantages?

Investigation 9.12 Patterns of change in mini-pond communities

One of the reasons for studying the growth of two populations together was to try to get a more realistic idea of what might actually happen when, and if, two populations interact in a natural community. It has been possible to study the interactions of populations which involve only the two populations under consideration. (In doing this it has been necessary to grow each population separately in order that the effect of one on the other can be judged.) Is this likely to be as simple in natural communities, or your mini-pond communities? If not, why not?

If your work on the mini-pond communities has begun to produce some results, discuss briefly any pattern of change which may be emerging. ▶ In view of the patterns of interaction studied in this section explain the changes as far as possible. Why must you be cautious in your explanations? ◀

This section began with a short account of the territorial behaviour of robins. What type of interaction between the members of the robin population is involved?

10 Particle interactions

In the previous section you investigated some of the interactions between fairly large building blocks. In this section the interactions are between particle building blocks (i.e. molecules, ions and atoms in giant structures).

You have already learnt that a small volume of particle building blocks contains millions of ions, atoms or molecules. And so, whereas in the previous section it was possible to consider interactions involving just a small number of building blocks, in this section it is impossible to isolate a single particle. It is the average behaviour of many millions of building blocks which you will be considering. Because of this, the predictions which can be made from the patterns are more precise.

The section is divided into three parts:
1 Particle interactions in solution.
2 Patterns of particle interactions.
3 New materials from particle interactions.

1 Particle interactions in solution

Before starting the investigations you should revise the meaning of the words 'solute', 'solvent' and 'solution'. Particles of solute will interact with particles of solvent to give a solution.

Investigation 10.1 Investigating solutions

Part a   Solid/liquid interaction

You will need

eight graduated test tubes, $20\,\text{cm}^3$ (or fewer if results are exchanged)
test tube rack
eight rubber bungs
wash bottle containing water at room temperature
spatula
graph paper
potassium chloride
access to balance

Pour 10 cm^3 of water into each of the graduated test tubes. Add the following (weighed) quantities of potassium chloride to each test tube:

test tube	mass of KCl/g	volume of solution /cm^3
1	1	
2	1.5	
3	2.0	
4	2.5	
5	3.0	
6	3.5	
7	4.5	
8	5.5	

Shake each test tube. Decide how you will know when no more solid will dissolve in the water. When no more of the potassium chloride will dissolve, measure the volumes of solution formed. (Note it is the solution volume only which you are measuring.) How accurate is each reading? Plot a graph of volume of solution against initial mass of potassium chloride.

Explain the shape of the graph and calculate from it the maximum amount of potassium chloride which will dissolve in 10 cm^3 of water at room temperature. How much potassium chloride will dissolve in 100 cm^3 of water at room temperature? ▶Use the kinetic theory to explain what is happening when a solute dissolves in a solvent. Are all solids soluble in water? ◀

▶What kind of graph would you expect to get for a sand/water system? Is it the same kind of interaction as the potassium chloride/water system? ◀

▷Part b   Liquid/liquid interaction

You will need

seven graduated test tubes, 20 cm^3 (or fewer if results are exchanged)
beaker, 50 cm^3
burette
retort stand, clamp and boss
test tube rack
seven rubber bungs
graph paper

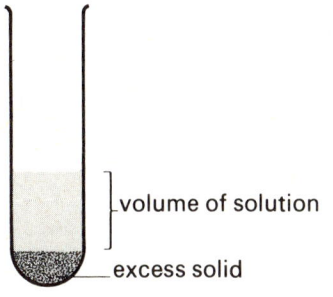

volume of solution

excess solid

Figure 10.1

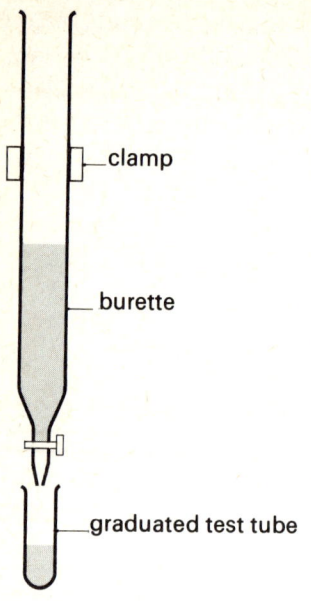

clamp

burette

graduated test tube

Figure 10.2

ethanol (dry)
wash bottle containing water at room temperature

Look at figure 10.3. What kind of graph would you expect to get when ethanol is added to water? (Remember that the sum of the two initial volumes of liquid is always 20 cm^3.)

Fill the burette with water. Pour ethanol from the beaker into each of the seven graduated test tubes. Each of the volumes is shown in the chart. Add the correct volumes of water from the burette. (Take your readings from the burette.) Shake the test tubes and find the final volumes of the solutions. How accurate are each of the readings? N.B. – You need to make very accurate measurements in this experiment.

test tube	volume of ethanol/cm^3	volume of water/cm^3	final volume of solution/cm^3
1	2	18	
2	5	15	
3	8	12	
4	10	10	
5	12	8	
6	15	5	
7	18	2	

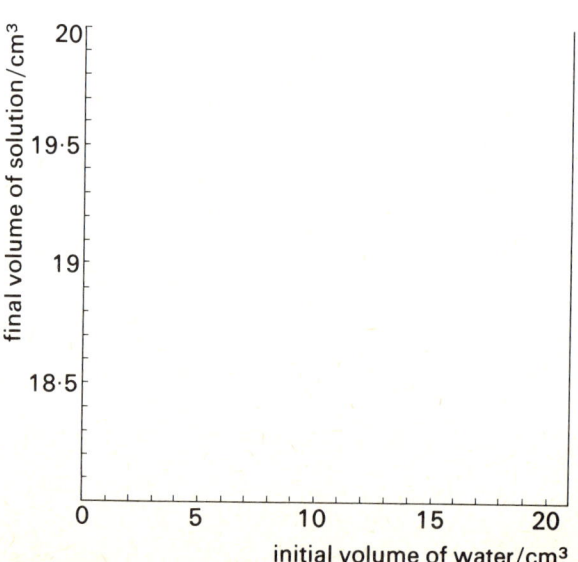

Figure 10.3

Plot a graph showing how the final volume of solution varies with the initial volume of water. What will be the final volume of solution when the initial volume of water is (i) 20 cm^3, and (ii) 0 cm^3? Is this the graph you expected to obtain? ▶Give an explanation for your results based on interactions between molecules. ◀

▷**Investigation 10.2 Dissolving salt in water**

This is a demonstration experiment in which the interaction between sodium chloride and water is investigated.

Investigation 10.3 Is solubility affected by temperature?

You will need

graph paper

▶Use the kinetic theory to predict whether you would expect the solubility of a solid in water to be affected by temperature. Does the table of solubility data below confirm your prediction?◀

| temperature/°C | some solubility data/g per 100 g of water | | | | | | | | | | |
	0	10	20	30	40	50	60	70	80	90	100
KCl	27.6	31.0	34.0	37.0	40.0	42.6	45.5	48.3	51.1	54.0	56.7
KClO$_3$	3.3	5.0	7.4	10.5	14.0	19.3	24.5	–	38.5	–	51.0
KNO$_3$	13.3	20.9	31.6	45.8	63.9	85.5	110.0	138.0	169.0	202.0	246.0
NaCl	35.7	35.8	36.0	36.3	36.6	37.3	37.5	37.8	38.4	39.0	39.8
NaNO$_3$	73.0	80.0	88.0	96.0	104.0	114.0	124.0	–	148.0	–	180.0
CuSO$_4$ anhydrous	14.3	17.4	20.7	25.0	28.5	33.3	40.0	–	55.0	–	75.4
K$_2$SO$_4$Al$_2$(SO$_4$)$_3$ 24H$_2$O	3.0	4.0	5.9	8.39	11.70	17.00	24.75	40.0	71.0	109.0	–
Na$_2$S$_2$O$_3$ anhydrous	52.5	61.0	70.0	84.7	102.6	169.7	206.7	–	248.8	254.2	266.0
Ca(OH)$_2$	0.185	0.176	0.165	0.153	0.141	0.128	0.116	0.106	0.094	0.085	0.077
CaSO$_4$	0.1759	0.1928	–	0.209	–	0.2097	0.2047	0.1974	–	–	0.1619
Ca(HCO$_3$)$_2$	16.15	–	16.60	–	17.05	–	17.50	–	17.95	–	18.40
NaOOC:CH$_3$:3H$_2$O	36.3	40.8	46.5	54.5	65.5	83.0	139.0	–	–	–	–
CaCO$_3$				0.0015 at 25 °C				0.0019 at 75 °C			

Use your table of data to show graphically how an increase in temperature affects the solubilities in water of each ionic giant structure:

a potassium nitrate

b sodium chloride

c calcium hydroxide.

Use the same graph paper for each solubility curve.

Do you notice anything of interest about these solubility curves?
▶ Suggest how it would be possible to purify sodium chloride (salt) by dissolving in water and recrystallising. ◀

So far you have been investigating solutions of solids in water and liquids in water. Solutions of gases in water, or gases in solids, or gases in gases, are all possible. Copy and complete the chart which follows:

solution	example (if solution is possible)
gas in gas	
gas in water	
gas in solid	
liquid in water	
solid in water	
solid in solid	
solid in gas	

Solvents other than water can be used, and experiments with 'non-aqueous' solvents are performed in the next experiment. All of the aqueous solutions you have used in this section have been poured down the sink, has this caused pollution? Would it be wise to pour the solvents used in Investigation 10.4 down the sink?

▷ **Investigation 10.4 Investigating solvents**

You will need

a range of solvents (e.g. water, ethanol, propanone and tetra-chlormethane)
a range of 'stains' (e.g. ink, fat and paint)
a range of materials (e.g. cotton, wool and nylon)

Investigate whether the solvents are useful for removing the various stains from different materials. Take great care when using the solvents.

Investigation 10.5 Are solutions homogeneous?

Use a dictionary to find the meaning of the word 'homogeneous'. (This word could have been used in Investigation 4.9.)
▶Devise and carry out an experiment to discover if a solution of sodium chloride/water is homogeneous. Would you expect all solutions to be homogeneous?◀

Investigation 10.6 Do temperature changes occur in interactions between solute and solvent?

You will need

0.1 mole of concentrated sulphuric acid (H_2SO_4)
0.1 mole of ammonium nitrate (NH_4NO_3)
0.1 mole of sodium chloride (NaCl)
beaker, 250 cm^3
thermometer ($-10\,°C$ to $110\,°C$)
measuring cylinder

N.B. – Concentrated sulphuric acid should be handled carefully.

Pour 100 cm^3 water into the beaker. Take the temperature of the water. Carefully and slowly pour the acid into the water, continuously stirring with the thermometer. Note the final temperature. Why would it be dangerous to add water to concentrated sulphuric acid (instead of acid to water)? Repeat the experiment for the other two substances. Do temperature changes occur in these interactions of solute and solvent?

▷Investigation 10.7 Getting mixed up!

This is a series of demonstration experiments on order and disorder.

Investigation 10.8 What happens to mass when interactions occur?

Already we have asked ourselves questions concerning energy (and, perhaps, disorder) in interactions. What about mass? Does this change when interactions take place?

You will need

conical flask, 100 cm^3
cork or rubber bung
glazed paper
potassium chloride (about 5 g)

Carry out experiments to obtain the following masses:
a mass of potassium chloride
b mass of about 50 cm^3 water
c mass of solution of potassium chloride in water.

What relationship is there between mass of solute and mass of solvent and the mass of solution? Was this true for the whole class? How accurate were your weighings? Can you be certain of your result?

2 Patterns of particle interactions

The particle interactions in Investigations 10.1–8 were interactions between solute and solvent. No new materials were formed (although giant structures were broken down).

A shorthand summary of one of the interactions is shown below:
aq + KCl(s) → KCl (aq)

This tells us that 1 mole of solid potassium chloride will dissolve in water to give an aqueous solution of potassium chloride. Write similar summaries for the other interactions. Shorthand summaries (or particle equations) can also be written when new substances are formed in particle interactions. For example, in Investigation 7.19 you found that copper and oxygen can interact to give black copper oxide:

i.e. copper + oxygen → black copper oxide.
►Use your results for Investigation 7.19 to write a particle equation for the interaction. ◄ (You will need the results to know how many moles of copper, oxygen and black copper oxide are involved.)

In order to write the equation you will need to use the abbreviation (g) for gas. (One further useful abbreviation is (l) for liquid.) At this stage you may wish to refer to the book *Chemical formulae and equations* in order to revise the use of the mole in calculations.

One important point to remember is that in *Patterns* the formula of a building block always represents one mole of that

24

building block. *It never represents a single particle.* Particle equations show how many moles of interacting particles are involved.

In the next investigation you will be working out more particle equations. But first, it is important to repeat an investigation like 10.9 for when new materials are found. Why is it important to repeat this investigation?

▶ **Investigation 10.9 What happens to mass when new materials are formed?**

Devise an experiment to discover the relationship between mass of reactants and mass of products in any one of the following three particle interactions:
a barium chloride solution and sodium carbonate solution
b iron filings and copper sulphate solution
c magnesium and hydrochloric acid.
(All solutions are aqueous.) What were the structures of the reactants and the products? ◀

Investigation 10.10 Particle equations: patterns of interaction

Part a   A reaction involving precipitates

You will need

six graduated test tubes, 20 cm³, in rack
glass rod
teat pipette
beaker, 100 cm³
Bunsen burner, tripod, gauze and asbestos square
1.0 M barium chloride and 1.0 M sodium carbonate
graph paper

Add 5 cm³ volumes of molar barium chloride solution to each of the graduated test tubes. Warm the test tubes and contents in a beaker of almost boiling water. Pour 2.0, 3.0, 4.0, 5.0, 6.0 and 7.0 cm³ of molar sodium carbonate into the six test tubes, stir the contents, remove from the beaker and allow to stand until the precipitates have settled (i.e. until the liquid is clear). Remove the test tubes and measure the volumes of the precipitates. Plot a graph using the axes shown on page 26:

What is the precipitate? (A flame test and the reaction with dilute acid will help you to decide.)

▶ Find out how many moles of sodium carbonate react with one

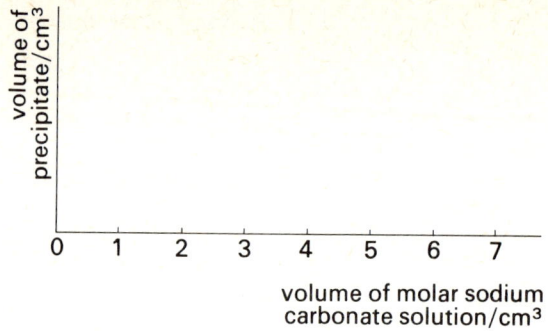

volume of precipitate/cm³

0 1 2 3 4 5 6 7

volume of molar sodium
carbonate solution/cm³

 mole of barium chloride. ◄ How does your answer compare with those obtained by other members of your class? ► Write a particle equation for the reaction. ◄

▷ Part b   A replacement reaction

You will need

two test tubes, 100 × 16 mm, in rack
test tube holder
glass rod
teat pipette
beaker, 100 cm³
spatula
Bunsen burner, tripod, gauze and asbestos square
access to balance
access to centrifuge
iron filings
copper sulphate (small crystals)
propanone
distilled water
knife

Dip the end of a knife blade into copper sulphate solution. What happens? In this experiment you are going to find out how many moles of copper are formed for every mole of iron that dissolves. Put about 2.5 g of copper sulphate crystals into a test tube and half fill it with distilled water. Warm it until the crystals have all dissolved. Cool the copper sulphate solution. Weigh about 0.5 g of iron filings into a second weighed test tube. Pour half the copper sulphate solution into the test tube containing the iron.

What happens to the colour of the solution? What happens to the iron filings? What happens to the temperature of the solution? Add the remains of the copper sulphate solution. Note what happens.

26

When the reaction appears to be complete, pour off most of the liquid (taking care not to pour off any copper). Add distilled water to wash the copper, centrifuge and then pour off the water. Repeat the washing, using propanone instead of water. Make sure the copper is well mixed with the propanone. After the last centrifuging, pour off the propanone and evaporate what remains by immersing the test tube for a few minutes in a beaker of near boiling water. Weigh the test tube and copper.

Look up the mass of 1 mole of iron and 1 mole of copper in a book of data. ▶ Then try to solve the problem, stated in the first paragraph, 'how many moles of copper are formed for every mole of iron that dissolves?' ◀ How does your answer compare with those obtained by other members of your class?

Part c   A reaction involving gases

You will need

two graduated test tubes, 20 cm^3
trough
two delivery tubes (one of which is large bore capillary tubing)
retort stand, two clamps and bosses
rubber tubing
rubber bung (single hole)
dropping pipette
100 mm magnesium ribbon
200 mm cotton
1.0 M hydrochloric acid
filter paper

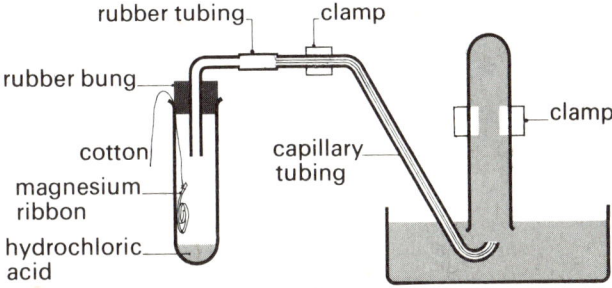

Figure 10.4

Use the dropping pipette to carefully measure 1 cm^3 of 1.0 M hydrochloric acid into the graduated test tubes. Weigh the magnesium ribbon and suspend it above the acid (see figure 10.4). When the air has finished bubbling through the capillary, clamp the second graduated test tube (filled with water) above the end of

27

the delivery tube. Tilt the first test tube so that the acid and metal interact.

When the interaction has finished, measure the volume of gas collected. What is this gas? What is the other product of this interaction? Wash, dry and weigh the remaining magnesium ribbon. What mass of magnesium interacted with the acid? ▶ How many moles is this? How many moles of acid were involved in the interaction? Knowing that 1 mole of a gas occupies a volume of 24 litres (at room temperature), how many moles of gas were formed? You should now be able to suggest an equation for this interaction. ◀ How does your equation compare with those obtained by other members of your class?

Particle equations are shorthand summaries of patterns of interaction. For example, whenever magnesium and oxygen interact to form magnesium oxide the summary of the interaction is always

$$2Mg(s) + O_2(g) \rightarrow 2MgO(s).$$

▶ The equation tells you nothing about the structures of the reactants and the product. What additional information would be needed to help you to decide this? ◀

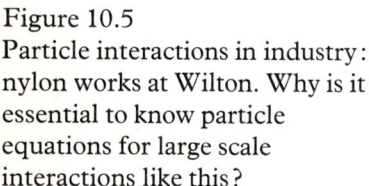

Investigation 10.11 Predictions from patterns

The interaction pattern for sodium and chlorine can be summarised as follows:

$$2Na(s) + Cl_2(g) \rightarrow 2NaCl(s).$$

Figure 10.5
Particle interactions in industry: nylon works at Wilton. Why is it essential to know particle equations for large scale interactions like this?

▶ Predict the mass of sodium chloride which would be formed from 2.3 g of sodium and excess chlorine. ◀ Was the same sort of prediction possible in the previous section 'Competition and predation'? ▶ Further problems on particle equations (including predictions) can be found in *Chemical formulae and equations.* ◀ From now onwards you should write equations for all particle interactions which are performed in the laboratory.

3 New materials from particle interactions

Investigation 10.12 Sulphuric acid

The Nuffield Chemistry background book *Sulphuric acid* gives an account of the history, manufacture and uses of sulphuric acid. The demonstration experiment shows how the acid can be made in the laboratory.

The following table shows the consumption of materials used for sulphuric acid manufacture.

	consumption of sulphur and other materials used for sulphuric acid manufacture/10^3 tonne				
period	sulphur	pyrites	spent oxide	anhydrite	zinc concentrates
1959	384	319	221	748	192
1960	440	353	251	760	198
1961	452	337	235	704	197
1962	461	318	210	862	227
1963	523	304	204	844	236
1964	599	288	204	943	257
1965	689	240	175	976	251
1966	636	239	172	979	254
1967	637	238	152	1 135	251
1968	660	217	114	1 258	320

Which was the most popular source of raw materials in 1968? Are any of the sources declining in popularity? Has the quantity of sulphuric acid manufactured during the period 1959–68 increased or decreased?

Part a   Concentrated acid

N.B. – Great care must be taken when experimenting with concentrated sulphuric acid. Your teacher will probably wish to perform this as a demonstration experiment.

You will need

safety goggles
two dry test tubes, 125 × 16 mm, in test tube rack
test tube holder
beaker, 100 cm³
evaporating basin
Bunsen burner
teat pipette
concentrated sulphuric acid
iron filings
filter paper
sucrose
small copper sulphate crystals

N.B. Concentrated sulphuric acid is a very dangerous chemical. You must always treat it with great care. Do not allow even one drop to touch you or the bench. Before carrying out experiments with the acid answer the following questions: Is the acid more or less dense than water? Is the acid viscous or mobile? What colour is the acid? Does the acid smell?

a With a glass rod put one drop of concentrated acid on to the centre of a piece of filter paper. Hold the paper so that the acid runs down. Does the acid have any effect on the paper? Drop the filter paper into water before throwing it away.

b Pour about 2 cm³ of concentrated acid into a dry test tube. Add the crystals of copper sulphate. What happens to the crystals? Pour the contents of the test tube into 50 cm³ water. What happens to the copper sulphate?

c Put about 2 g of sucrose into the evaporating basin. Add about 1 cm³ of concentrated acid. What happens?

d Pour about 2 cm³ of concentrated acid into a test tube. Add a few iron filings. Gently warm the test tube. What happens?

There is a pattern in the behaviour of sulphuric acid in experiments (i)–(iv).

Part b   Properties of dilute sulphuric acid

You will need

safety goggles
four test tubes, 125×16 mm, in test tube rack
Bunsen burner
dilute sulphuric acid
magnesium ribbon, iron filings, granulated zinc, copper turnings
and lead foil
copper oxide, magnesium oxide and zinc oxide
sodium hydroxide solution
sodium carbonate, calcium carbonate, magnesium carbonate and
copper carbonate
universal indicator

Investigate the reactions between dilute sulphuric acid and the range of substances listed above. You should summarise your results in a table. What patterns are there in these interactions? ▶ Write particle equations for the interactions which occur. ◀ You could note the acidity (pH) of the colourless solutions at various stages of the interactions. Use reference books to discover some of the uses of sulphuric acid. Would you say that it is an important chemical?

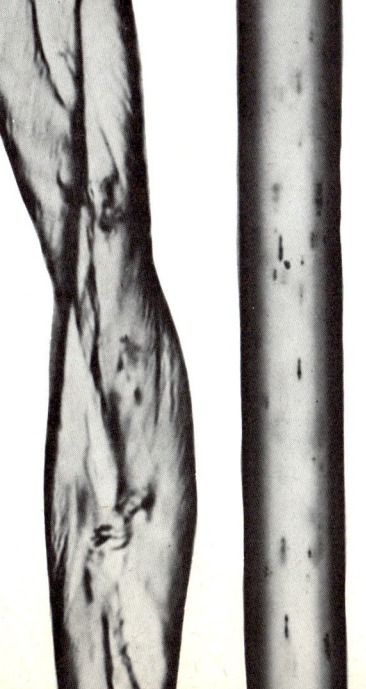

Figure 10.6
Compare the photograph of the natural polymer (a) with that of the man-made polymer (b)

Smaller molecules can interact with each other to give much larger molecules. Two examples of such interactions are shown below:

a $A + A + A + A \rightarrow A - A - A - A$

Separate molecules of A join together to give one long chain (which investigation did you perform where this happened?)

b $H \wedge\!\wedge\!\wedge H + HO \wedge\!\wedge\!\wedge OH \rightarrow H \wedge\!\wedge\!\wedge\!\wedge OH + H_2O$ then
$HO \wedge\!\wedge\!\wedge OH + H \wedge\!\wedge\!\wedge OH + H \wedge\!\wedge\!\wedge H \rightarrow HO \wedge\!\wedge\!\wedge\!\wedge\!\wedge\!\wedge H + 2H_2O$

and so on. The product eliminated need not necessarily be water: any small molecule can be removed.

One of the interactions is called 'condensation' and the other is called 'addition'. Which description best fits the pattern of interaction (a) and which description best fits the pattern of interaction (b)? Both interactions are termed 'polymerisation' and the very large molecules which are formed are called 'polymers'. Plastics are polymers. (When have you met the reverse interaction whereby large molecules are broken down into smaller molecules?)

Investigation 10.14 Plastics

Part a Condensation polymers

You will need

two test tubes, 125 × 16 mm
teat pipette
stirring rod
formaldehyde solution (formalin)
urea
concentrated sulphuric acid

Pour about 5 cm^3 formaldehyde solution into a test tube. Add urea and stir until no more will dissolve. The clear solution should then be poured into the second test tube. Add four or five drops of concentrated sulphuric acid to the mixture and stir with a glass rod. Describe what happens. ▶Why has this happened? What is the structure of the product?◀ The plastic you have made can be baked.

Another plastic, nylon, can be made by your teacher. What are the uses of nylon?

Part b Addition polymers

You will need

hard glass test tube, 125 × 16 mm, with cork and delivery tube
test tube, 100 × 16 mm
beaker, 100 cm^3
Bunsen burner, tripod, gauze and asbestos square
stand and clamp
access to oven
chips of Perspex (about 5 g)
lauroyl peroxide (about 0.02 g)

Put a few chips of Perspex in a test tube with a side-arm and connect a delivery tube to it. Warm the test tube with a non-roaring flame and collect the distillate in a cooled test tube. ▶Why do you think that the distillate has smaller molecules than the original Perspex? Warm the distillate in an oven at 80 °C for nine to ten hours. What happens? Can you explain this?◀

The second reaction can be speeded up by adding a speck of lauroyl peroxide as a catalyst. Find out how long the reaction takes when the catalyst is present. It might be useful to digress for a lesson and investigate the action of another catalyst.

Investigation 10.15 Another look at a catalyst

You will need

conical flask, 100 cm^3, wide neck, with bung and delivery tube
measuring cylinder, 25 cm^3
trough
stopclock, or watch, with seconds hand
graph paper
spatula
test pipette, with 1 cm^3 graduation
graduated test tube, 20 cm^3
20-volume hydrogen peroxide
manganese dioxide

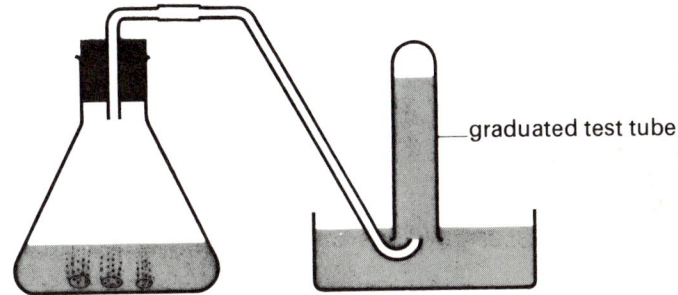

graduated test tube

Figure 10.7

Add 2 cm^3 of the hydrogen peroxide solution to 48 cm^3 of water in the flask (figure 10.7). Add one half a spatula measure of manganese dioxide and immediately insert the bung. Start the stopclock and note the time taken to collect 0, 5, 10, 15 and 20 cm^3

of oxygen. Plot a graph showing the volume of oxygen produced against time.

What effect does a catalyst have on the rate of a reaction? ▶ Investigate the effect (a) of varying the concentration of hydrogen peroxide, and (b) of varying the quantity of manganese dioxide. ◀ (You could also try the reaction with a drop of fresh blood instead of manganese dioxide. Here the catalyst is an enzyme.)

▷**Investigation 10.16 Experiments with plastics – identification of fibres**

Figure 10.8
Crimplene and silk dress

Part a   Using Shirlastain

You will need

piece of 'Shirley' multifibre fabric strip
samples of different undyed materials from home
Shirlastain 'E' solution
Bunsen burner, tripod, gauze and asbestos square
beaker, 500 cm³ (or source of warm water)
beaker, 250 cm³
tongs or forceps
stirring rod

N.B. – It is important not to allow the stain to get into contact with clothes or skin.

Different fabrics are stained different colours by the Shirlastain 'E' solution. Gently boil the Shirlastain 'E' solution (stirring all the time) and then immerse the multifibre strip for two minutes. Use tongs or forceps to remove the fabric from the stain and rinse the sample in warm water (which is either in a large beaker or is allowed to run from the tap).

The multifibre strip contains bands of fibres in the following order: red border and black index thread; cotton (natural cellulose); viscose rayon; wool; silk; cellulose secondary acetate; cellulose triacetate; Nylon 6.6; Nylon 6; Terylene; Acrilan 1656; Courtelle; Orlon; red border.

Draw a table to show the colour each strip is stained. This is a classification pattern. ▶ Now can you identify the fabrics from home, following the same procedure as that for the multifibre strip. ◀

How could you check whether the fabric worn by the model in figure 10.8 was woven from one or two man-made materials? (If two materials have been used, one might form the weft and the other the warp.)

Part b   Burning

You will need

crucible tongs
Bunsen burner and asbestos square
samples of different material

Hold small pieces (about 1 cm squares) of each of the samples in the Bunsen flame. Identify each of the samples using the pattern shown in the table which follows:

material	reaction
cotton viscose rayon	smell of burning paper, burns vigorously
wool silk	smell of burning hair, does not burn vigorously
cellulose secondary acetate cellulose triacetate	smell of vinegar, easily crushed black solid formed, burns, fabric shrinks from flame
Nylon 6.6 Nylon 6	smell of burning hair, hard black solid formed, burns with difficulty, fabric shrinks from flame
Terylene	the same as nylon; black smoke
Acrilan 1656 Courtelle Orlon	easily crushed black solid formed, burns with sooty flame, fabric shrinks from flame

Of what use are these identification experiments? When might it be necessary to carry out identifications such as these?

Investigation 10.17   Problems of disposal

Look at the two photographs (see figures 10.9 and 10.10). What differences are there in the types of rubbish? Read the articles which follow and collect any other statements. Discuss the problems of disposal.

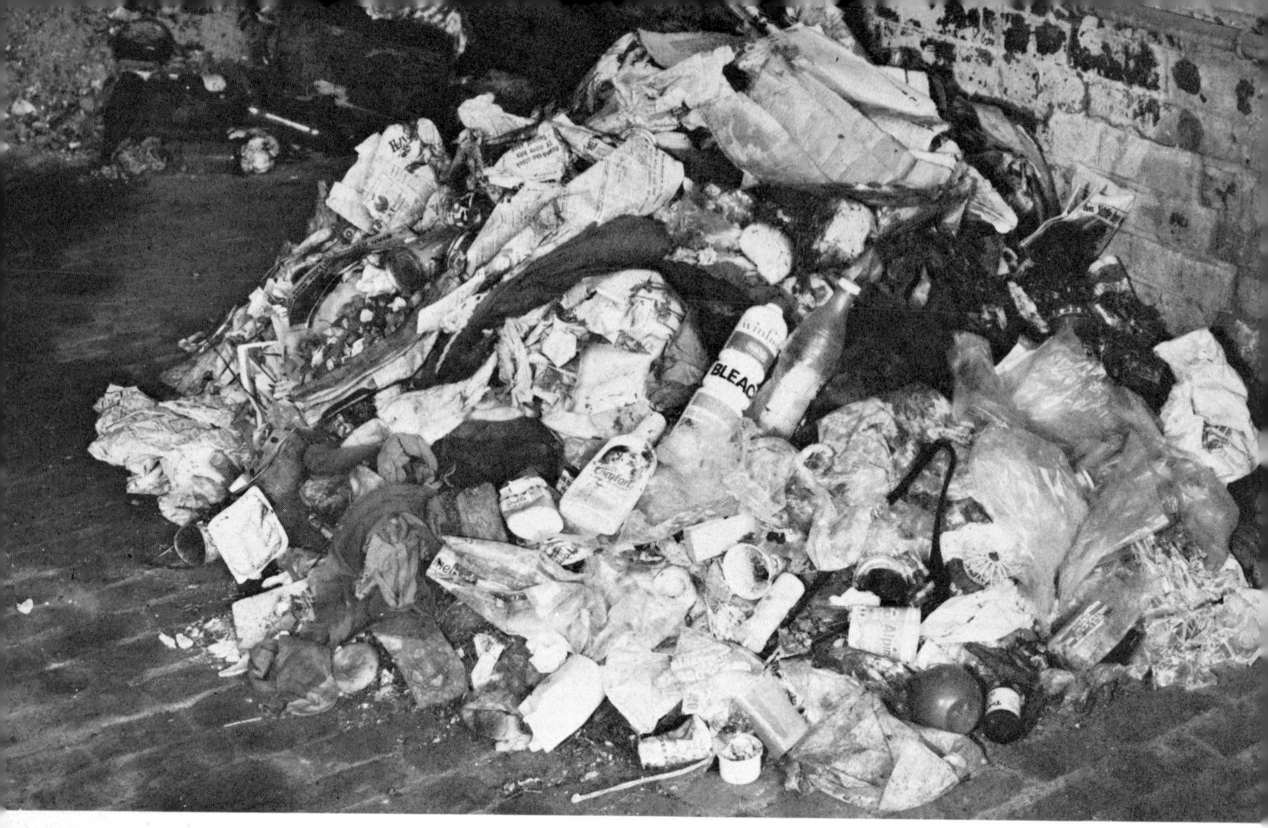

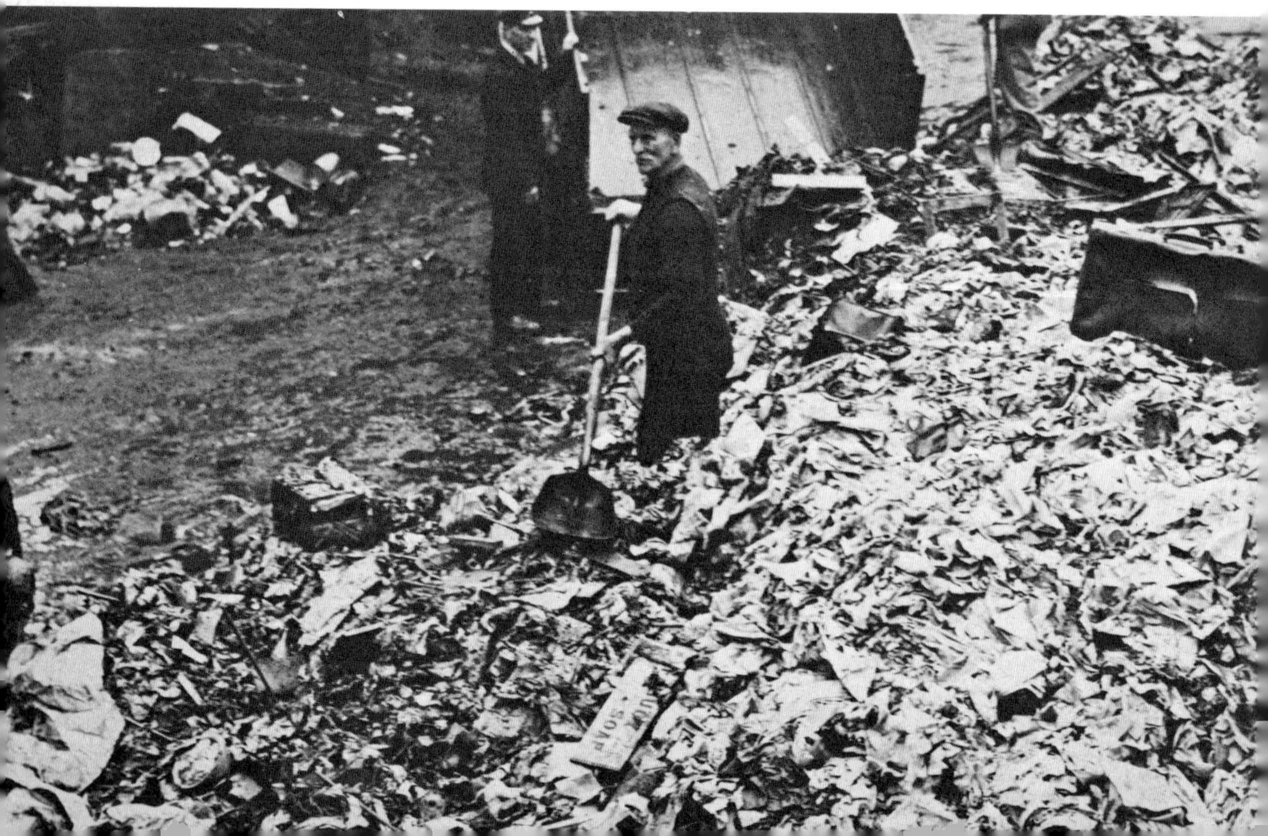

Figure 10.9
Rubbish of today

Figure 10.10
Rubbish of 40 years ago

Waste plastic could be used as fuel

BY OUR SCIENCE CORRESPONDENT

Plastic waste and litter in Britain will rise from 250,000 tons this year to about $1\frac{1}{4}$ million tons in 1980.

According to a monograph published by the Society of Chemical Industry, and introduced at a seminar in London yesterday by its author, Dr J. J. P. Staudinger, the increase will present no serious problems, provided that the public pays for new methods of disposal as required, while also developing greater conscience about national tidiness.

The packaging industry can help by marketing designs which, like the new plastic quart milk bottle, can be easily crushed by hand into a small volume.

The trouble with plastic is its bulk and permanence, and the best disposal methods so far devised are either baling or some form of incineration. In free tipping, currently the most widely used method of disposal, plastic can cause drainage and stability problems. But highly compressed bales with a high plastic content can be extremely useful in land reclamation and infilling.

Concern

Authorities engaged in producing useful compost from garbage are watching the plastic non-returnable bottle situation with some concern.

But, as Dr Staudinger pointed out, one ton of plastic possesses the energy equivalent of three tons of fuel oil and this property could be turned to advantage. Instead of composting or direct incineration, pyrolisis disposal, producing gas suitable for inclusion in the town supply or the production of electricity via turbines, might be a valuable future answer.

In spite of panic in the US about the production of hydrochloric acid during the burning of PVC, this was not a real problem provided that smoke scrubbing devices were installed.

Disposal of Plastics Waste and Litter: SCI Monograph, £2.

'DOOMWATCH' MENAC[E]

Top scientist warns of the plastic peril

A SCIENTIST warned yesterday of the dangers of developing "Frankenstein" bugs to destroy waste plastics.

Plastics consultant Dr Peter Staudinger said that the bugs could destroy telephone systems, radar—and even the space programme.

The idea of plastics which eventually destroy themselves—thus solving waste and litter problems

—formed the plot of a recent BBC TV Doomwatch thriller programme.

Dr Staudinger, of the Society of Chemical Industry, told a "clean-up" conference at Leeds that plastics did not decompose.

Scientists had three ideas for altering this: Modifying plastics, creating self-destructive materials, or using micro-organisms to "chew up" the material.

Creature

But, he said: "I hope such a Frankenstein creature will never appear."

One result could be that housewives would find lemonade and other plastic bottles disintegrating in their shopping bags.

Afterwards, Dr Staudinger explained: "So far we know of no bugs that attack plastic, although it contains carbon, which is a nutrient.

"But if these were developed it would be catastrophic. They would ruin our existence. Nobody should try this technique.

"It would be impossible to control such bugs. They would ruin radar stations, telephone systems, underground cables and even the space programme."

THE SUN, Wednesday. April 15, 1970

Investigation 10.18 'The Polythene Story'

This is printed in the book *Science and decision-making*.

Discuss the advantages (particularly in the home) of artificial fibres and plastics.

DRAWN BY DENNIS COLLINS—WRITTEN BY MAURICE DODD

In Section 9 it was necessary to have control experiments. Why were control experiments not usually necessary in this section? Both Sections 9 and 10 were concerned with interactions of building blocks. What other differences between the two sections (apart from control experiments) did you find interesting?

11 Electrical interactions

In Sections 9 and 10 you considered interactions between building blocks of similar types. Sometimes these interactions led to changes in the building blocks themselves. For example, populations change in size, and molecules can be changed to other molecules.

In this section interactions are also studied, but the building blocks involved are not altered. In fact for this section you do not even need to know which building block is involved, only that an electric current can be thought of in terms of the movement of charged particles. What are the charged building blocks you have met already? Which of them in movement would constitute an electric current? Electric currents are not visible. Suppose you connect a piece of wire to a dry battery (see figure 11.1). How can you tell whether an electric current is flowing in the wire? There are several answers, but they all show that it is possible to detect only the effects of electric currents, and not the currents themselves. What are the main effects of electric currents?

Figure 11.1

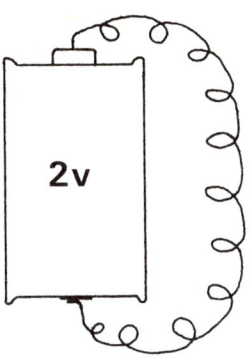

Investigation 11.1 Doing without electricity

Electricity is something we all tend to take for granted – that is until we have to do without it! Figure 11.2 on page 40 shows some of the common devices which use electricity. Each of these depends on the patterns of this section. How were the same jobs done before electricity was available? Were any of these jobs impossible?

Early in 1972 a strike of coal miners meant that there were frequent power cuts and supply reductions. Why did a strike of coal miners cause an electricity shortage? The use of electricity for advertising was banned and most street lights were switched off. In each area different times of different days were designated as times of Low Risk (cuts or reductions unlikely), Medium Risk (reductions possible) or High Risk (cuts almost certain). Certain small areas were excluded from cuts or reductions because they contained such buildings as hospitals. Why is it important that hospitals should not have electricity cuts? The worst people had to suffer was a three-hour cut in the morning and another in the evening.

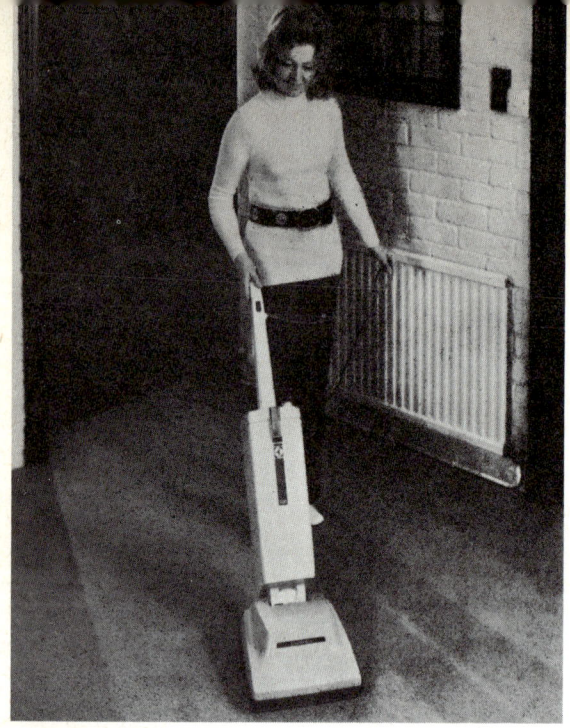

Figure 11.2

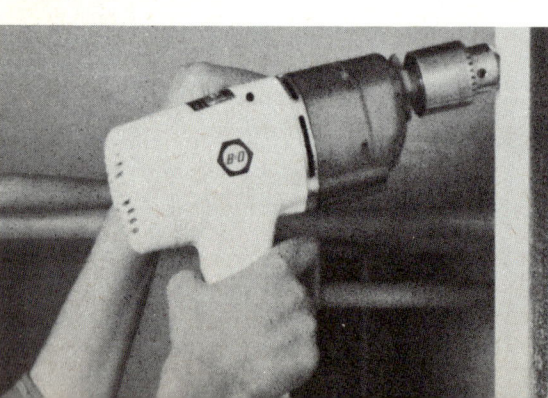

Figure 11.3

Blackouts will total nine hours daily

By HAROLD JACKSON

The Central Electricity Generating Board announced last night that disconnections would increase from 10 per cent to 15 per cent from this morning. The high risk areas will now spend nine hours without electricity.

The industrial effects of the miners' stoppage became graver yesterday. As the miners presented their case to the Wilberforce inquiry and the Prime Minister called in both sides of industry for consultations, the number of workers made idle by the power crisis rose by 50 per cent.

The Department of Employment estimated that 1.2 million workers were laid off during the day—half as many again as the day before—and employers were warned by the Generating Board that increases in the working hours on days when power was available could only hasten a total shutdown. Yesterday's figures mean that in the first two days of the emergency measures, the number of people unemployed in Britain has doubled.

The Midlands was again badly affected by the power cuts and ICI announced that it had given a week's notice to nearly half its labour force, about 60,000 people on weekly wages.

The Generating Board said that it not only had to make the rota disconnections yesterday but it had also had to reduce voltage by six per cent from lunchtime onwards. From this morning, however, high risk areas which have only been blacked out for two of the three peak periods would now lose their power for the whole risk period.

POWER POINTS

AN advance warning five minutes before a power cut is being given to Londoners by the London Electricity Board.

SMASH and grab raiders in Liverpool are cashing in on cuts and raiding shops.

CANDLES were lit before the Royal Investiture at Buckingham Palace yesterday—in case of blackouts, but were not needed and flickered unnoticed alongside electrically lit candelabra.

DERBY Education Committee yesterday ordered all schools —more than 100—in the borough to close for the rest of the week.

VIGILANTE residents in Worthing, Sussex, have compiled a blacklist of 40 shops which keep lights on at night and threaten to boycott them.

TWINS—Sharon and Shayne Gladden were doing fine yesterday after being delivered by ambulance men, Michael Welsh and John Robinson, when a cut put Mrs Janet Gladden's home in Ipswich in darkness.

COUNCILLORS at Wolverhampton are annoyed at a plan to spend £1,500 to buy 30 cylinder gas heaters to keep town hall staff warm.

THE YOUTH Campaign of Help the Aged said yesterday that its fund-raising activities for old people in need are being severely curtailed by the power crisis.

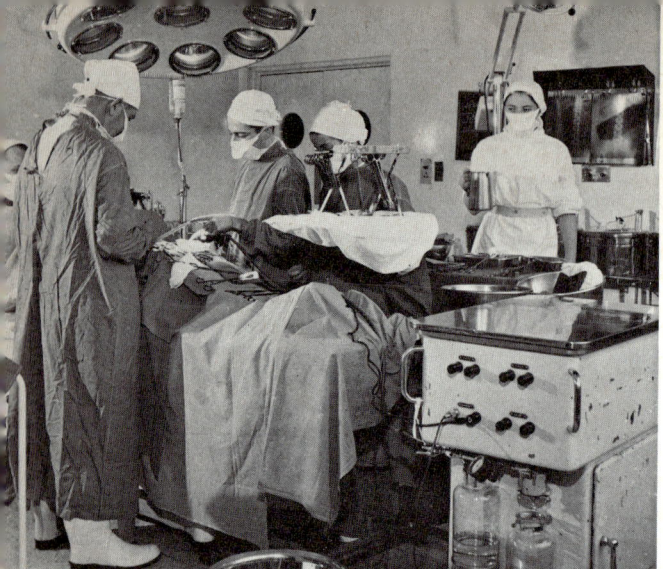

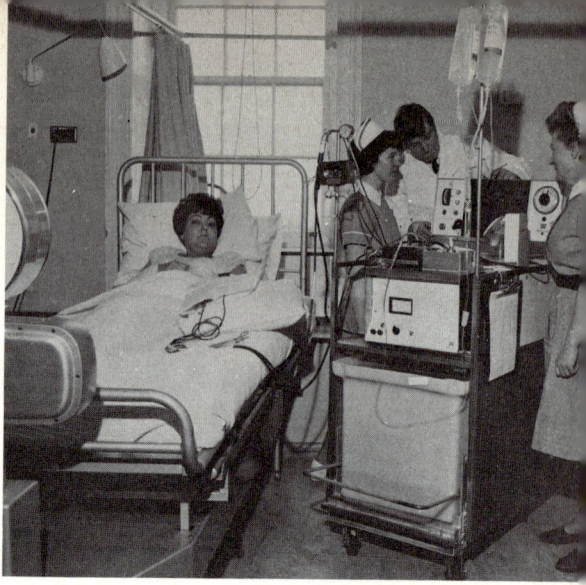

Figure 11.4
a An operating theatre

b Modern hospitals have many electrical devices used to monitor and treat patients. That shown is a kidney machine

Discuss the effects on your life of doing without electricity for:
1 three hours
2 a day
3 a week
4 a year.

Most of these effects are disadvantages: are there any advantages?

Figure 11.5

Apart from equipment for heating and lighting, most of the electrical devices we use depend on electrical interactions involving magnetism. They include such things as a hair drier, door chimes, an electric guitar, a loudspeaker, a transformer and a foodmixer. You will be studying these interactions in this section and will be able to make some of the devices mentioned.

Investigation 11.2 Magnetism from electricity

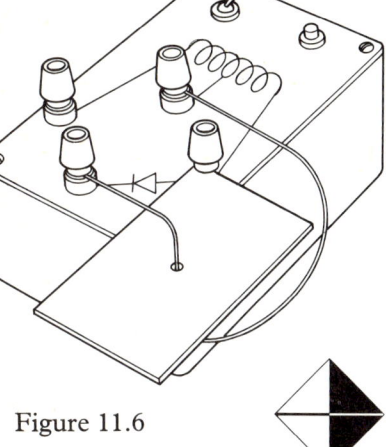

Figure 11.6

You will need

low voltage, high current supply unit (d.c.) (as illustrated in figure 11.6)
fine iron filings in sprinkler
plotting compass
single strand insulated copper wire
card
sheets of various materials

Part a

A plotting compass indicates the direction of a magnetic field. The speed of its oscillation also gives some idea of the strength of the field. Use the compass to search for patterns of magnetism near a wire carrying a current. Investigate the effect of reversing the current and of putting the wire horizontally above and below the compass.

▷ Part b

Investigate the effect of placing different materials between the wire and the compass. Try to find which stops the effect, or reduces it considerably.

▷ Part c

Repeat part a using iron filings instead of a compass, and note whether the pattern is the same. What is the 'shape' of the magnetic field? How does the strength vary with distance from the wire?

Part d

Now go on to investigate more complex situations. Several are

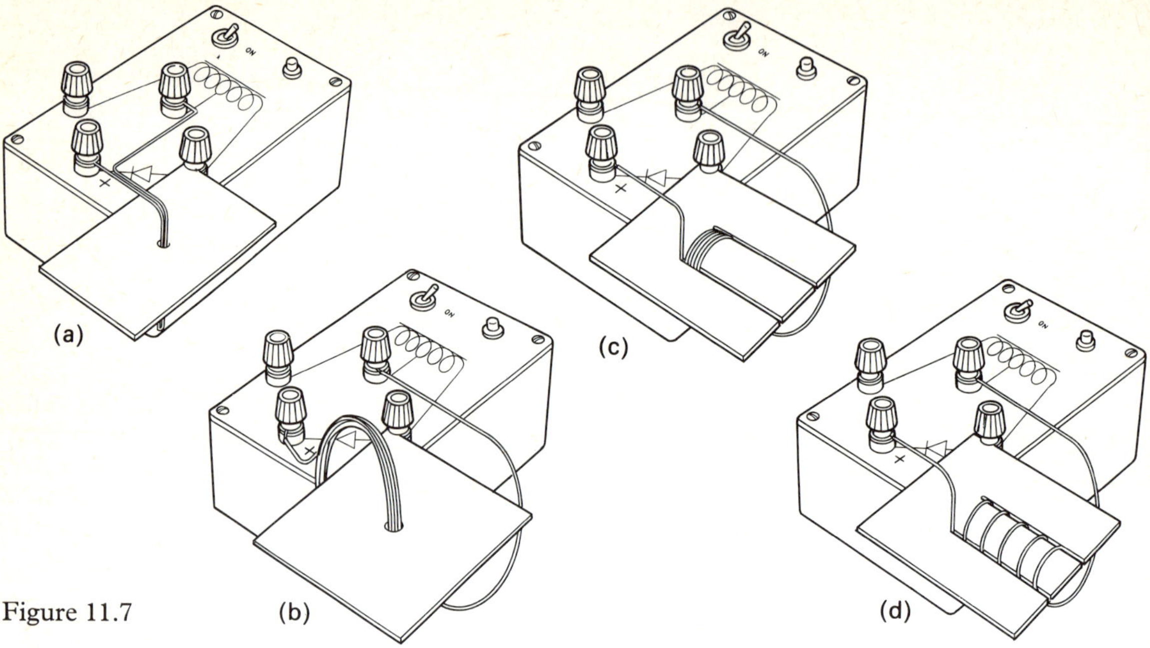

(a)

(b)

(c)

(d)

Figure 11.7

Figure 11.8.

illustrated in figure 11.7. In each case predict what would happen and test your prediction. If you have time investigate the pattern of the magnetic field produced outside and inside long coils. (Use a pencil or a larger cylinder as a former on which to wind the coils.)

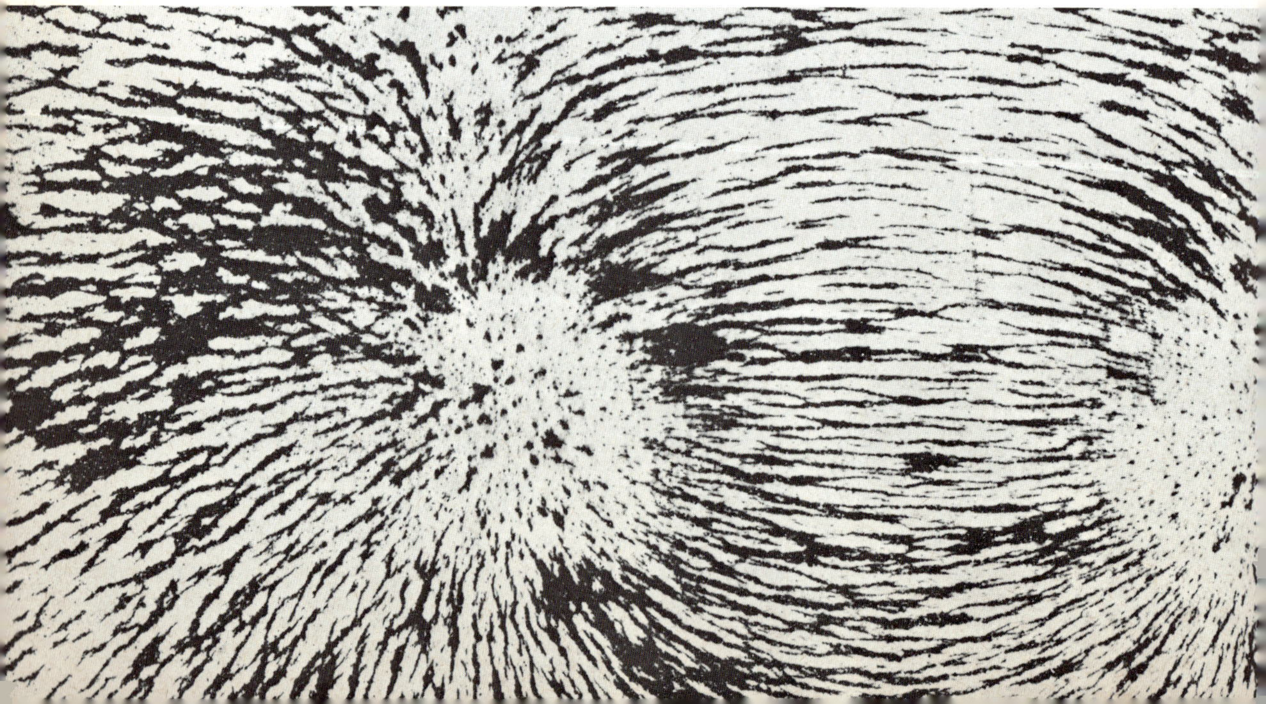

Part e

▶ What arrangement of currents would produce the magnetic field pattern illustrated in figure 11.8? ◀

▶ The magnetic field pattern shown is that of a bar magnet. Discuss whether a suitable arrangement of electric currents could be a model to explain the magnetism of a permanent bar magnet. If so, what charged particles could make up the current? ◀

▷ **Investigation 11.3 Magnetic field patterns of magnets**

You will need

fine iron filings in sprinkler
 Magnadur magnets (flat)
Ticonal magnets (bar)

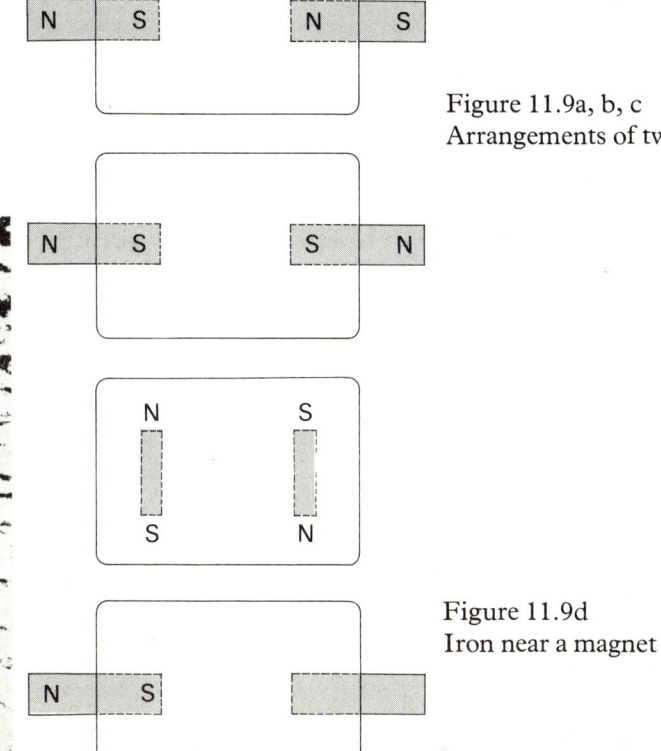

Figure 11.9a, b, c
Arrangements of two magnets

Figure 11.9d
Iron near a magnet

card
pieces of soft iron

Use the pattern of attraction and repulsion to locate the poles of the various sorts of magnet. You do not need to know which pole is which. (If you did need to know, how could you find out?)

Use iron filings to investigate the patterns of magnetic field:

1 near a single magnet (try each sort in turn)
2 near two magnets of the same sort in the arrangement shown (see figure 11.9a–c on page 45)
3 near a magnet and a piece of iron as shown (see figure 11.9d on page 45)
4 if you have time, near other simple arrangements of magnets.

Investigation 11.4 Electromagnets

Part a   Making an electromagnet

You will need

low voltage, high current supply unit (d.c.)
C-cores
former for winding coils
single strand insulated copper wire
iron nails or tacks
rods or bars of various substances

▶In Investigation 11.2 you found that a current in a coil produced a magnetic field. You detected this field by means of the forces on a plotting compass and on iron filings. Using the same electric circuit find a way of making the magnetic force on pieces of iron much stronger without altering the circuit at all. What other ways are there to increase the force using the same current? Use your answers to design, make and test an electromagnet. ◀

▷Part b   Using an electromagnet to measure current

▶Devise a way of using an electromagnet to show how great the current is which flows through it. Draw a diagram of your suggestion. Construct it if there is time. In order to obtain a reading of the current in amps, what would you need to do? Using your design, would it be possible to tell which way the current was passing? ◀

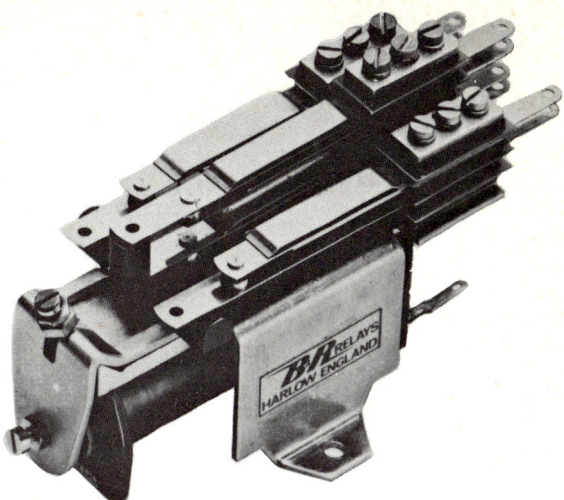

Figure 11.10b
A relay, in which an electromagnet operates a
switch or switches

Figure 11.10a
The force exerted by an
electromagnet can be
considerable

▷Part c   Other uses of electromagnets

Make a list of as many situations as you can where electromagnets
are used in some form. The pictures in figure 11.10 show a few.
Use your list in writing an illustrated essay on 'Modern applications
of electromagnetism and permanent magnetism'.

State the pattern which you have found relating electric currents
and magnetic fields (including the effect of iron).

Part a

Magnets produce magnetic fields and exert forces on each other. Currents also produce magnetic fields, so one might ask if a magnet exerts a force on a current. Devise an experiment to investigate this interaction. Does its direction depend on the directions of the magnetic field and the current? If so, in what way? The diagrams (see figures 11.11 and 11.12) may help you.

You will need

low voltage, high current supply unit (d.c)
magnets (flat or bar)
single strand insulated wire

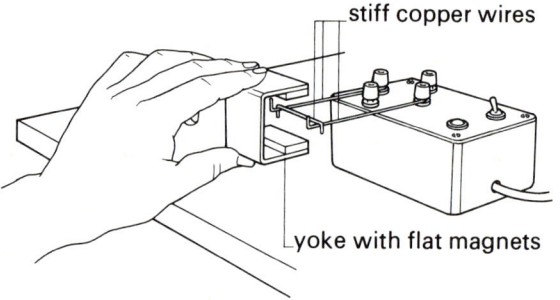

Figure 11.11
Using magnadur (flat) magnets

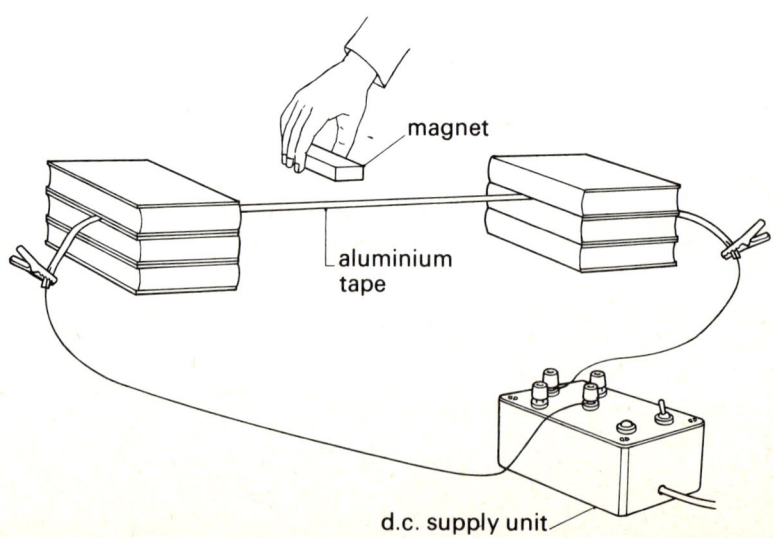

Figure 11.12
Using ticonal (bar) magnets

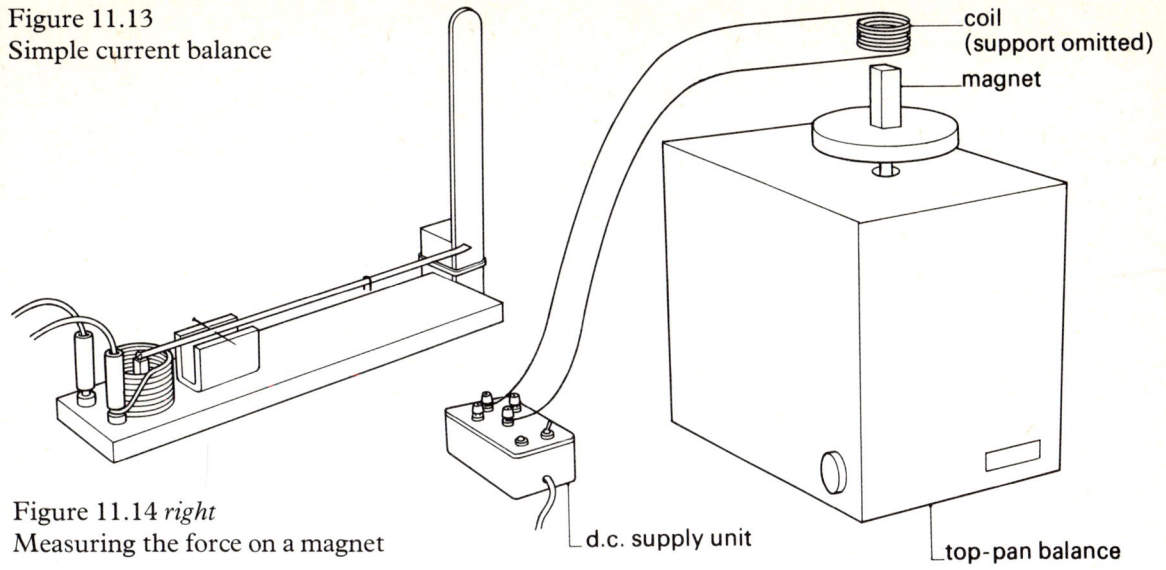

Figure 11.13
Simple current balance

Figure 11.14 *right*
Measuring the force on a magnet

coil
(support omitted)

magnet

d.c. supply unit

top-pan balance

You may need

aluminium tape
crocodile clips
steel yoke
stiff copper wire

Part b

You may have done an experiment previously to investigate the reverse interaction, the force a current exerts on a magnet. Figure 11.13 shows one form of the apparatus which you can use yourself. Another way to do the experiment is shown in figure 11.14. What can you say about the direction of this force?

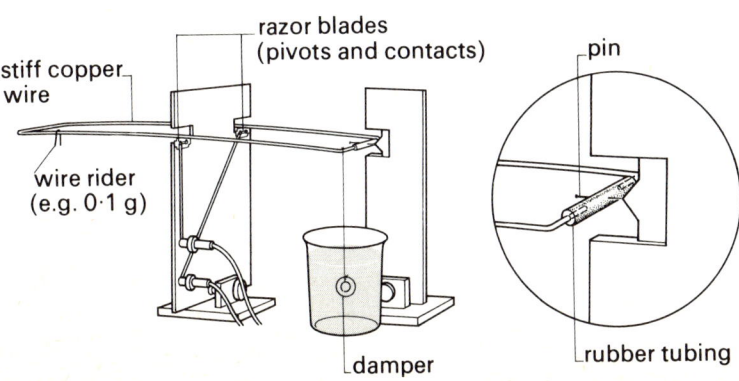

razor blades
(pivots and contacts)

pin

stiff copper
wire

wire rider
(e.g. 0·1 g)

damper

rubber tubing

Figure 11.15
Measuring the force on a current

49

Part c

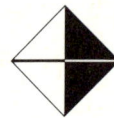 ▷Investigate how the forces in a and b depend on the current. Does doubling the current double the force? Investigate also the effect of a stronger magnetic field. Figure 11.15 suggests one way to approach this.

What pattern relating current and magnetic field can you state as a result of doing this investigation? Your statement of the pattern will possibly include the word 'interaction' (or 'interact'). Explain why this word is particularly useful in this pattern.

Part d

▶You have found that interactions occur between charges in motion and magnets. A piece of copper wire can be thought of as a giant structure composed of positive ions (strictly many linked structures) together with electrons. Explain the fact that moving a copper wire along its length near a magnet produces no interaction. (The answer is not that it is moving much slower than the charges in the wire you have been using.)◀

Investigation 11.6 Moving coil meters

Part a

You will need

low voltage, high current supply unit (d.c.)
armature
base
magnadur (flat) magnets
rivets
single strand insulated copper wire
split pins
steel yoke
rheostat
drinking straw

▶Make a simple moving-coil meter based on the pattern of interaction you found in Investigation 11.5. The diagrams shown in figure 11.16 should help you. (Your apparatus may be slightly different from that illustrated, but the principle will be the same.)◀

▶When you have made your meter work, answer the following questions. What makes the coil move? What makes it stop moving?

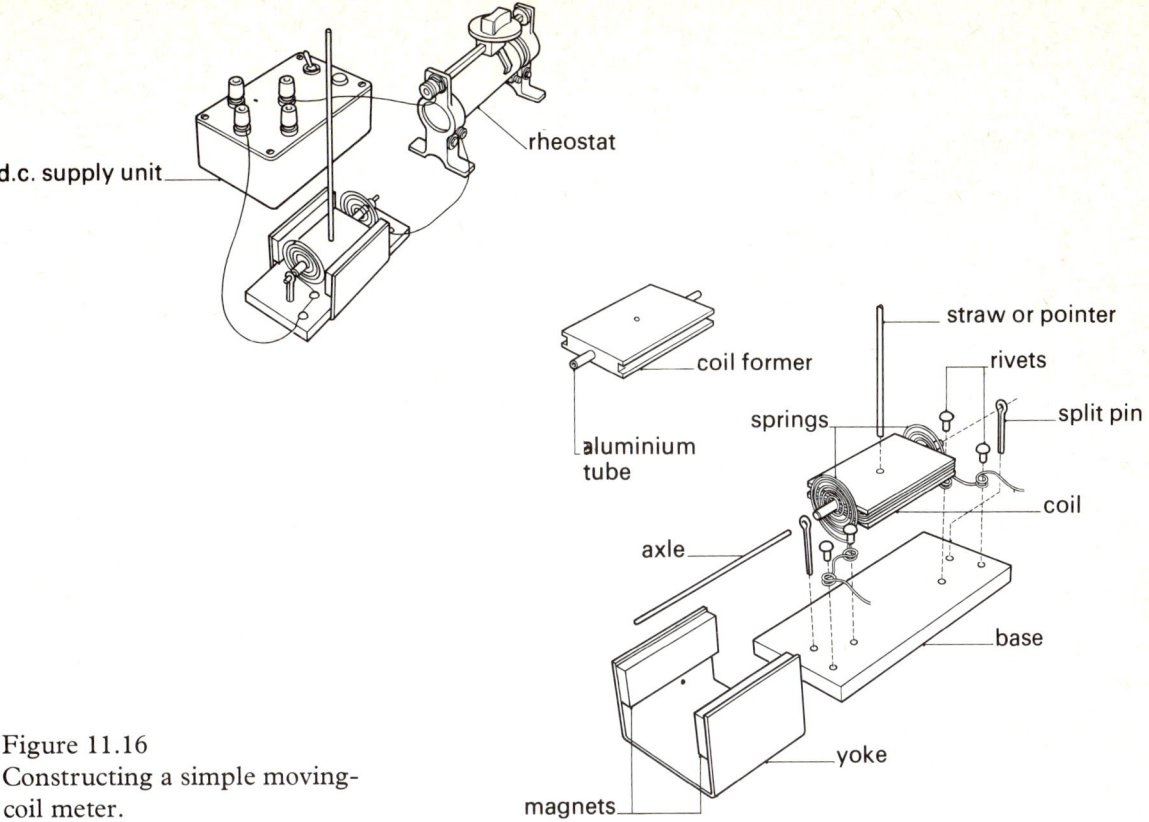

d.c. supply unit

rheostat

coil former

aluminium tube

springs

axle

magnets

straw or pointer

rivets

split pin

coil

base

yoke

Figure 11.16
Constructing a simple moving-coil meter.

What is the best position for the coil before any current is passed, if the instrument is to be used with currents in either direction? What is the best position if it will only be used for currents in one direction? ◀

Part b

Compare your meter with several commercial moving-coil meters, and make a note of the similarities and differences. Figures 11.17–20 show some of the modern developments in meter technology. The centre-magnet movement is both cheaper and less bulky than the traditional sort. What is the advantage of the 240° movement?

Part c

▷Moving-coil meters are used in a wide variety of different situations where the information needs to be available continuously.

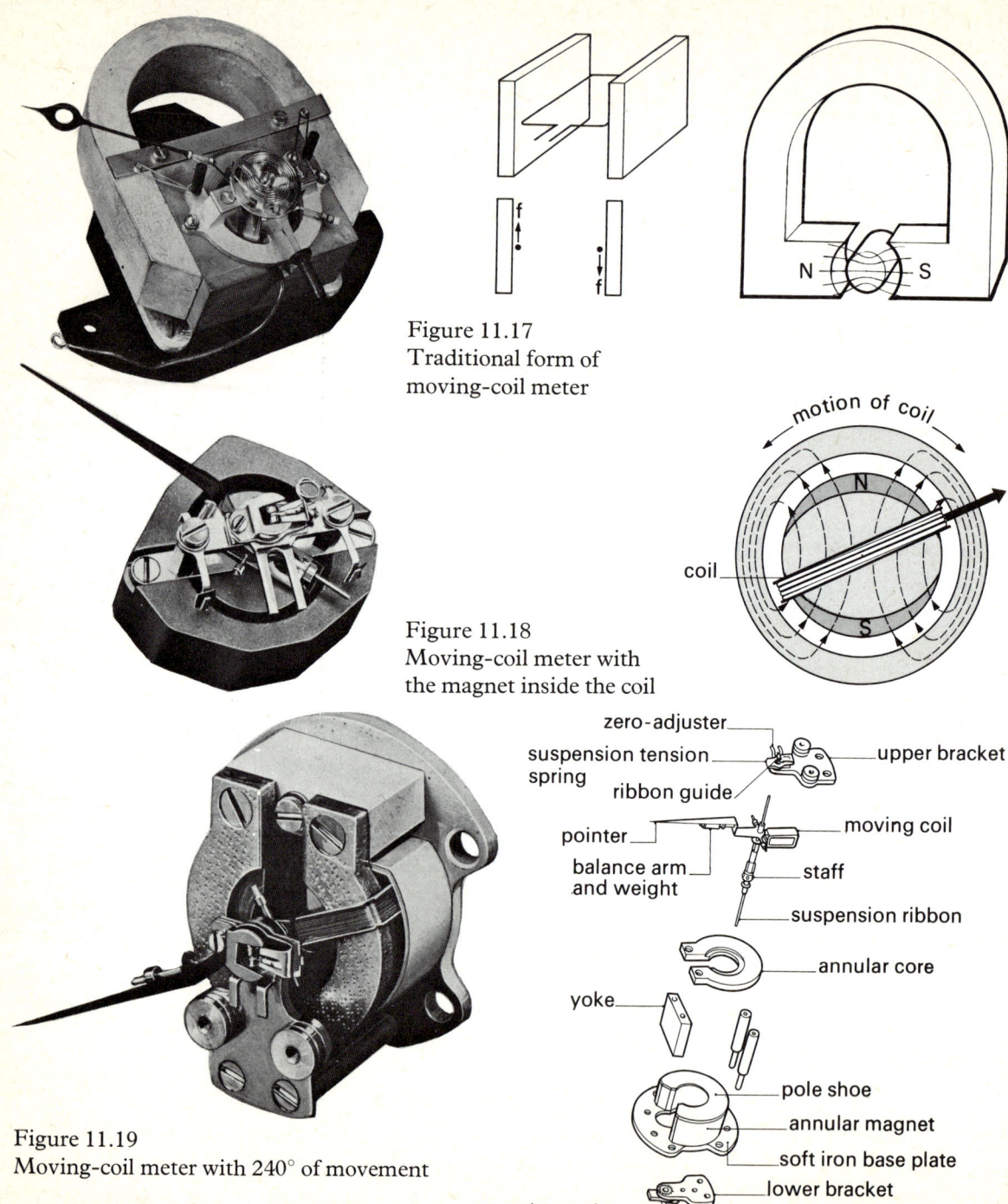

Figure 11.17
Traditional form of
moving-coil meter

Figure 11.18
Moving-coil meter with
the magnet inside the coil

motion of coil

N

S

coil

Figure 11.19
Moving-coil meter with 240° of movement

zero-adjuster
suspension tension spring
ribbon guide
upper bracket
pointer
moving coil
balance arm and weight
staff
suspension ribbon
annular core
yoke
pole shoe
annular magnet
soft iron base plate
lower bracket
tension spring

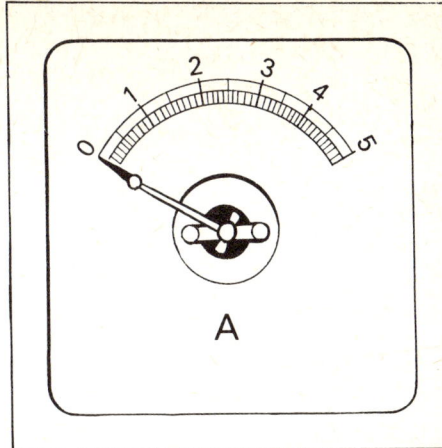

Figure 11.20
240° and 120° scales of the same
length

Figure 11.21
This control unit in a modern
steel works uses many moving-
coil meters to show a variety of
measurements

Figure 11.22
The pilot of an aircraft needs
information from a large number
of moving-coil meters

Figures 11.21 and 11.22 show two of these. Discuss what differences would be made to our lives if we did not have cheap, convenient and reliable measuring instruments.

Investigation 11.7 Electric motors

Part a

You will need

low voltage, high current supply unit (d.c.)
moving coil meter constructed in Investigation 11.6
cellulose tape
valve rubber cut into rings

▶The patterns used in making the moving coil meter can also be used to make a motor. What differences are needed? Uncoil the springs, so that the wires to and from the coil are loose and do not restrict its movement. Now what happens when you pass a current through the coil? What happens when you reverse the current? How could you make the motor rotate continuously in one direction and not just oscillate back and forth? Use your answers to these questions to turn your meter into a motor which will work on direct current. The diagram (see figure 11.23) should help. Be particularly careful about the electrical contact between the ends of the coil and the wire 'brushes'. ◀

Figure 11.23

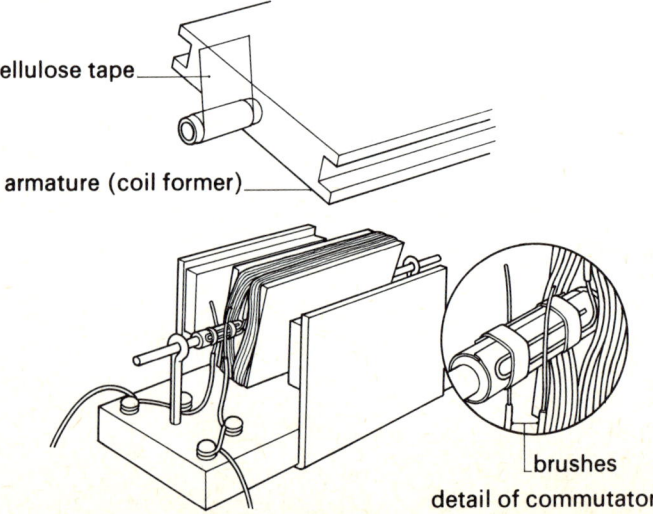

cellulose tape

armature (coil former)

brushes
detail of commutator

▶When you have made your motor work, answer the following. What is the best position for the armature to be in when the current through the coil changes direction? (If your motor does not work very well, it may be because you had not thought about this question.)◀

Part b

Compare your motor with several commercial ones, looking particularly at the armature, commutator and magnet(s). Make a note of the similarities and differences, and use these to suggest what might make the commercial motors more efficient than the one you have made.

Part c

Electric motors are used for many purposes, but most of them operate from alternating current (a.c. – see Investigation 11.8). The main direct current (d.c.) motors are those operated from batteries and those used for driving electric trains (see the *Patterns* topic book, *The electrification of British Rail*). Make a list of the possible uses of d.c. motors in an expensive car. Which motor in any car requires the greatest current?

Investigation 11.8 Alternating current

Part a   A.c. or d.c.?

This demonstration illustrates how a.c. (alternating current) differs from d.c. (direct current), and how an oscilloscope can be used to 'draw a graph' of an alternating current. Describe alternating current in terms of the charged building blocks involved.

Part b   Does a bicycle dynamo produce a.c. or d.c.?

When you understand the controls on the oscilloscope, use the instrument to answer this question.

Part c   What sort of motor would work on a.c.?

▶Suggest one answer to this problem by using the patterns you have found in this section.◀ Electric motors for domestic purposes are usually of this sort. (There are several other types of a.c. motor which work in rather different ways.) Make a list of the domestic applications of electric motors (a mail-order catalogue might help). The photographs in figure 11.2 will give you a start.

▷Part d   A.C. meter

▶Design, and if possible construct, a simple meter based on the magnetic effect of a current, which will work with both a.c. and d.c. ◀

▷Part e   Non-magnetic meters

Suggest an arrangement which could form the basis of a non-magnetic measurement of current. Work out a simple design. Would it work with a.c. or only d.c.?

Investigation 11.9 Motors and people

In a previous investigation you considered the wide variety of domestic appliances in which electric motors are used. A significant proportion of our income is spent on electrical goods. The following table shows the ownership of several items in different countries. Discuss possible reasons for the differences. Discuss possible consequences of people having few electrical goods.

| country | percentage of households owning this item | | | |
	vacuum cleaner	electric refrigerator	washing machine	dish washer
Great Britain	84	58	64	1
France	53	80	77	3
West Germany	87	85	69	—
Netherlands	100	78	87	4
Italy	—	83	63	7
USA	92	100	92	26
Sweden	89	92	80	6
Switzerland	95	91	46*	6
Japan	55	78	81	—
Finland	62	76	16	1
Belgium	64	63	64	—
Spain	—	42	—	—
Canada	81	—	83	—

*85 per cent have access to a washing machine

56

Are there any disadvantages for people in owning large numbers of electrical appliances? (For example, do they exaggerate social differences? Do they make people too 'soft'?) The table below shows how the ownership of food and drink mixers has grown in recent years. Estimate how long it might be before the market is saturated, i.e. no increase in ownership can be expected.

households owning food/drink mixers in UK							
year	1964	1965	1966	1967	1968	1969	1970
percentage	6	9	11	13	18	22	24

▷ **Investigation 11.10 Do magnetic interactions only happen with currents in wires?**

So far you have investigated currents in wires, usually of copper. This is not surprising: most electric currents do flow in copper wires. But there are other possibilities. One of these you met in Section 8 'The electron, ions and giant structures'. Discuss examples of electric currents in something other than a wire. Design and perform experiments to answer the question in the title. In each case describe the current in terms of the movement of building blocks.

Suppose in one case you found no result. How sure could you be that there is no interaction? Why is a negative result of an experiment never as conclusive as a positive result? Does the pattern which applies to currents in wires apply also to currents elsewhere?

Investigation 11.11 Two electric currents

Magnets produce magnetic fields and exert forces on each other. A current produces a magnetic field and exerts a force on a magnet, and the magnet also exerts a force on the current. Does any interaction (force) exist between two electric currents?

Part a

Devise an experiment to investigate such an interaction including whether the direction of the force depends on the directions of the currents. In designing the experiment remember (a) the strength of the magnetic field of a current of a few amps in a wire, compared to that of a permanent magnet, and (b) the approximate size of the force which exists between a permanent magnet and such a current. Are you looking for large or small forces?

Part b

▶Consider two parallel wires, A and B, carrying currents in the same direction. Work out the direction of the force which this magnetic field would produce on the current in wire B. Figure 11.24 may help. ◀

Figure 11.24

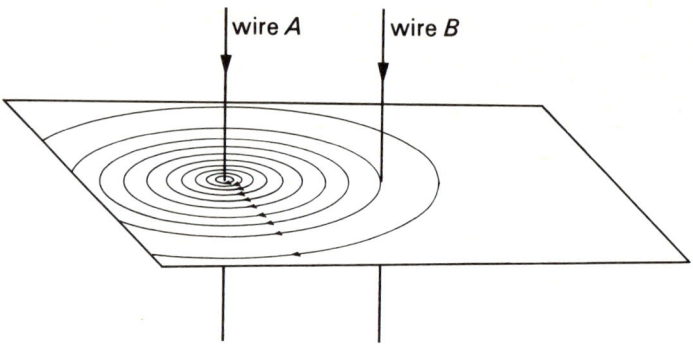

▶In a similar way you can work out the direction of the force on A produced by the magnetic field of B. ◀ Compare your results with what you found in the experiment in part a.

Part c

(A more difficult experiment.) Investigate how the force depends on the current. For example, does doubling the current double the force? The apparatus shown in figure 11.14 or 11.15 could be modified for this purpose.

Part d

The interaction between two currents is the basis of the definition of one ampere (A, the unit of electric current). When two long parallel wires exactly 1 m apart in a vacuum each carry a current of exactly 1 A, then the force on each is 2×10^{-7} N for each metre of its length. (N is the abbreviation for newton, the unit of force.)
▶Suppose two parallel cables each carried 1 000 A d.c. (a.c. would be more usual, but there is a d.c. link under the channel to France.) If the cables were in air, which is not for this purpose

significantly different from a vacuum, what would be the force on 1 m of one cable due to the other? (Think out first what would happen if one cable carried 1 000 A and the other 1 A. What would you assume about:

a how the magnetic field depends on the current
b how the force depends on the current and on the magnetic field?) ◄

Consider whether the answer you obtain would present any problems for the engineers. If so, why? If not, why not?

▷Part e

Like an electric current, a magnetic field is something you cannot observe directly. You can observe its effects. Could this investigation be explained in terms of the interactions between building blocks, without using the concept of magnetic field? Could the previous investigations be explained without this concept?

Investigation 11.12 Electricity from magnetism

The basic patterns concerning the interactions of magnets with other magnets and with magnetic materials were stated by Peter Peregrine in 1269, following experimental investigations (it was unusual for experiments to be done at that time).

Electromagnetism was not discovered until 1820, when the three patterns you have met were found:

electric current → magnetic field   I (Oersted, 1820)

magnetic field
+   } → force   II (Ampére, 1820)
electric current

electric current
+   } → force   III (Ampére, 1820)
electric current

Michael Faraday (1791–1867) was well aware of these effects. (His experiments in the nineteenth century are recognised as an outstanding contribution to our understanding of electricity. For more details see the Nuffield Chemistry background book and the *Jackdaw* about him.) Faraday was convinced that these patterns implied the existence of the reverse effect:

magnetic field → electric current

For ten years he thought about this prediction and carried out experiments to verify it, but without success. He tried many experiments, but found that a stationary magnet, or a steady current, never seemed to give the pattern for which he was searching. Eventually, however, he found what he was looking for, and in 1831 he wrote:

> . . . it appeared very extraordinary, that as every electric current was accompanied by a corresponding intensity of magnetic action at right angles to the current, good conductors of electricity, when placed within the sphere of this action, should not have any current induced through them, or some sensible effect produced equivalent in force to such a current.
>
> These considerations, with their consequence, the hope of obtaining electricity from ordinary magnetism, have stimulated me at various times to investigate experimentally the inductive effect of electric currents. I have lately arrived at positive results . . .

(*Experimental Researches*, Vol. I, first series: 3, 4)

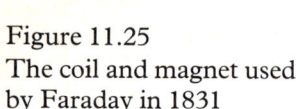

Figure 11.25
The coil and magnet used by Faraday in 1831

Faraday did not have the convenient sources of current and strong magnets that we have. If he had, he would certainly have spent much less than ten years on his search. With these advantages over Faraday, you should be able to find one form of the pattern.

Part a

You will need

C-cores and clip
galvanometer
magnets
pieces of iron
single strand insulated copper wire
steel yoke

Devise experiments to find the pattern of magnetism giving rise to electric currents. The diagram (see figure 11.26). will help you. When is a current produced? What does the current strength depend on?

The current produced is called an induced current and the process is called electromagnetic induction. State the pattern of electromagnetic induction. If possible, put this pattern in terms of building blocks.

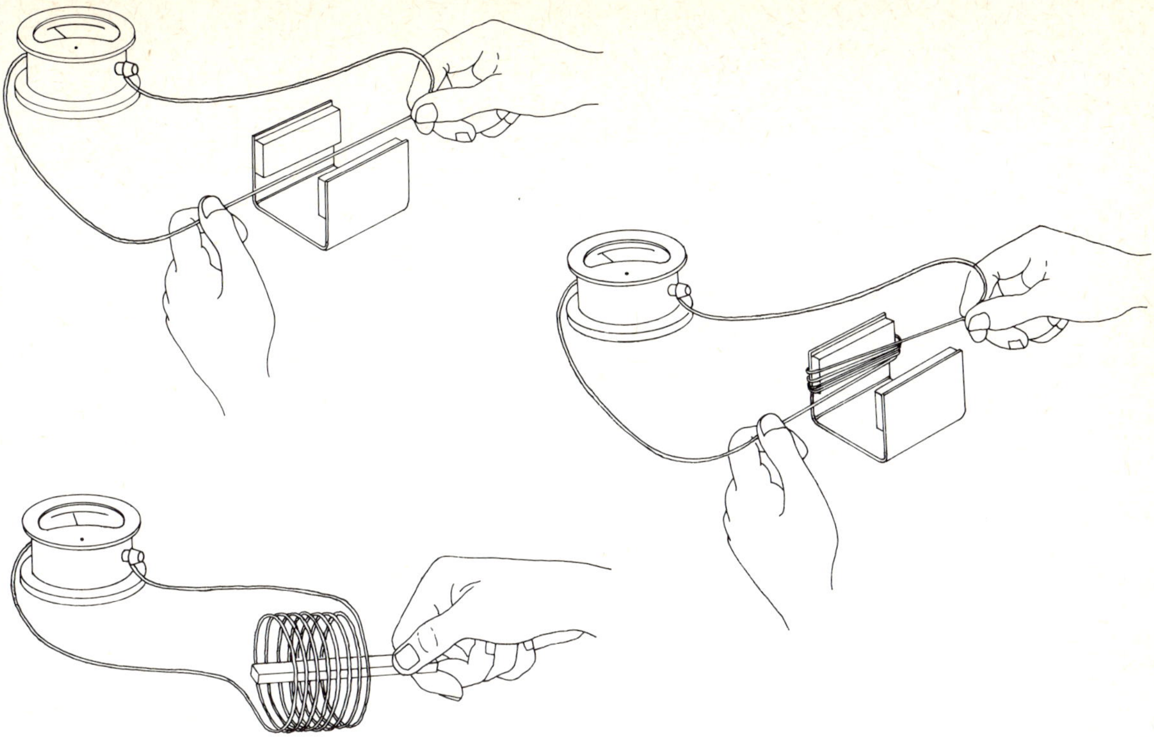

Figure 11.26

Part b

▶ Predict what you expect to happen when a bar magnet is brought near to an iron C-core with a coil (about 20 turns) on it as shown in figure 11.27. What difference will the position of the coil make? What do you expect when the magnet is pulled off again? What about keeping the magnet still and moving the C-core and coil? Test all these by experiment. ◀

Figure 11.27

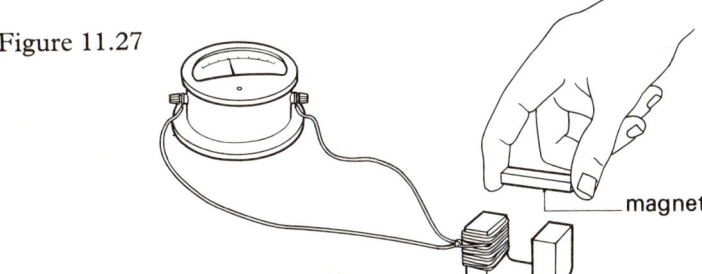
magnet

C-core

▶ Now predict and test what would happen if the coil is first placed round the magnet, and the C-core is then brought to it. ◀

Part c

▷Place a piece of iron across the magnet poles, and then move the coil near the magnet as shown in figure 11.28. Does it make any difference to the current induced if the coil is round the iron or not? What modification to the pattern emerges from this?

Figure 11.28

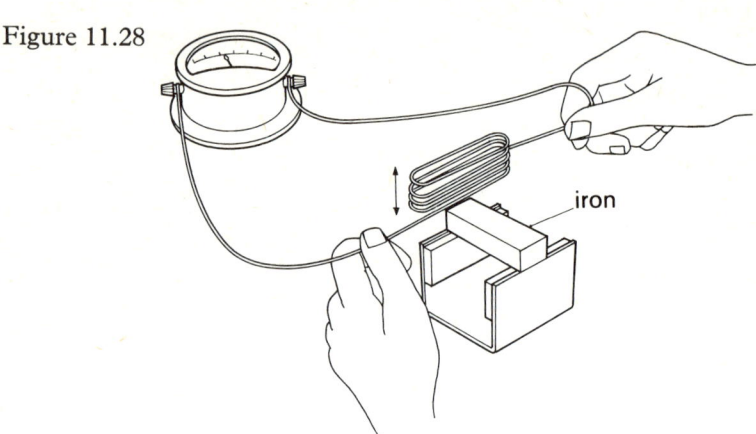

iron

Investigation 11.13 Can the simple electric motor work in reverse?

Figure 11.29
a The completed motor showing the brush connections

Part a

You will need

the electric motor you made previously
galvanometer

b A method of spinning the motor

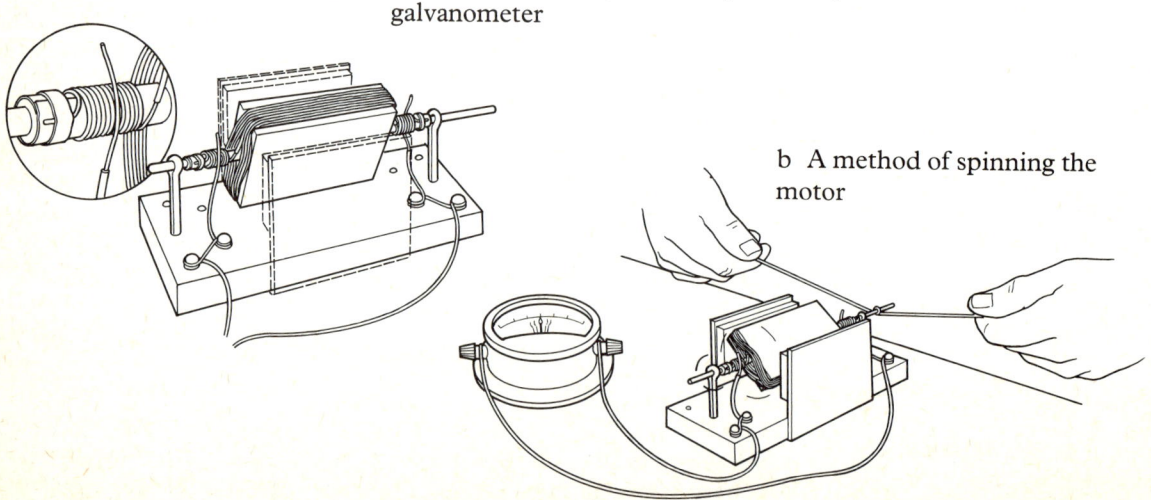

▶This problem does not mean 'can you make your motor spin backwards'. (What two different ways could you use to do that?) Normally an electric motor is driven by an electric current. Can you use your motor to produce (it would be better to say induce) an electric current? Make any necessary changes, and test whether it works. Does it produce a.c. or d.c.? Modify it to produce the other. What two names are used for a motor working in reverse?◀

Part b

You will need

electric motor (d.c., commercially made)
d.c. supply
ammeter   to suit motor
connecting wire
switch

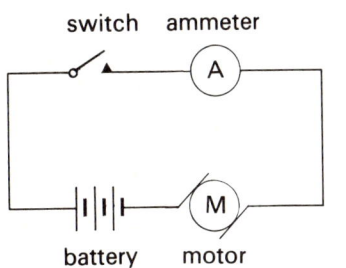

Figure 11.30

You have seen that rotating the armature of a motor by hand makes it work as a generator. Does an electric motor work as a generator while it is operating normally as a motor? If the motor were to act as a generator, do you think the induced current would help or hinder the current from the battery? This experiment should help you to find the answers to these questions. Connect up a motor to a suitable battery (or d.c. supply) and ammeter (see figure 11.30).

Measure the current when the motor is running freely. ▶Would the motor act as a generator if the armature was not rotating?◀ Stop the rotation, and see what difference it makes to the current. You should now be able to answer the questions posed at the beginning of part b. What pattern do you find in the direction of the induced current?

Part c

▷ *Additional requirement*

rheostat

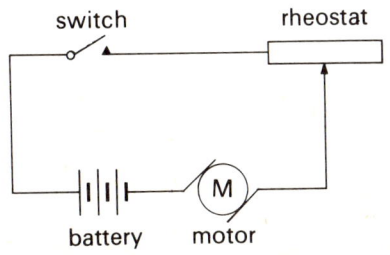

Figure 11.31

When the armature is not rotating the current can be so much larger than when it is rotating. This is quite a problem when large motors are being started. Explain why. How could the circuit shown in figure 11.31 be used to overcome the problem? Try it out if possible.

Investigation 11.14 Can currents produce electromagnetic induction?

You will need

dry cell
low voltage supply unit (a.c.)
C-cores and clip
galvanometer
rheostat
single strand insulated copper wire
switch

Part a

Wind a coil of about ten turns on a C-core and connect it through a switch to a dry cell. This is the primary circuit. The switch should be turned off when you are not experimenting. Wind a coil of about twenty turns on the other C-core, and connect it to a galvanometer. This is the secondary circuit.

▶Predict what would happen if you bring the primary coil and core (with the current on) near to the secondary coil and core, and if you take them away again. Test your predictions. Predict and test the effect of moving the secondary coil and core, keeping the primary coil and core still. ◀

Part b

Clip the cores (with coils) together. ▶Predict and test the effect of (a) switching on and (b) switching off the primary circuit. What movement of the primary core and coil produces the same effect as switching it on? Explain your answer. ◀

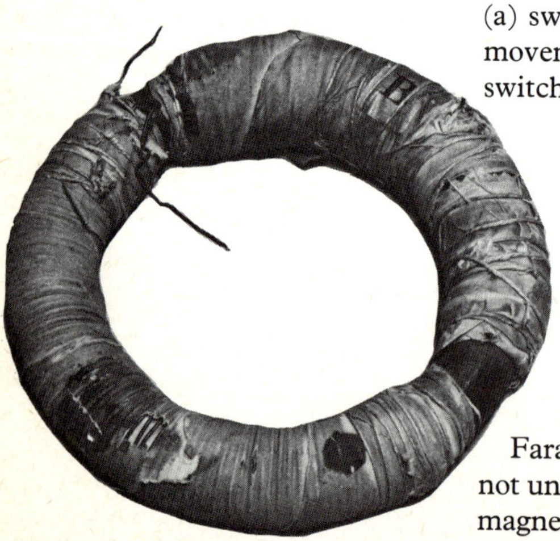

Figure 11.32
Faraday's iron ring wound with two coils of copper wire

Faraday did an experiment like this on 29 August 1831. It was not until 1 October the same year that he used a coil and permanent magnet as in Investigation 11.12a. (For more details see the Longman Physics Topics book *Electromagnetism*.)

Part c

Add a rheostat to your primary circuit as shown in figure 11.33.
▶ Predict and test the effect of (a) increasing and (b) decreasing the primary current by means of the rheostat. Predict and test the effect of continually increasing and decreasing the primary current. ◀

Figure 11.33

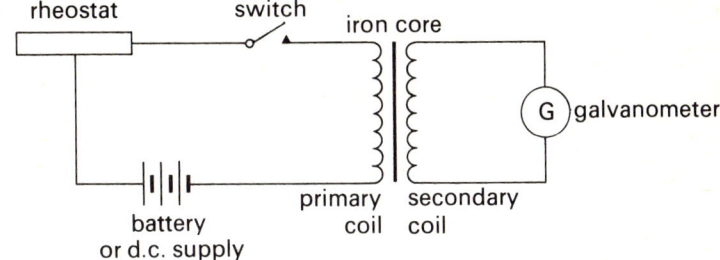

Part d

▶ Use the results of part c to predict what would happen if you passed a.c. through the primary coil. Why would the galvanometer not be a suitable instrument to detect a.c.? Set up the circuit shown in figure 11.34 to test your prediction. ◀

Figure 11.34

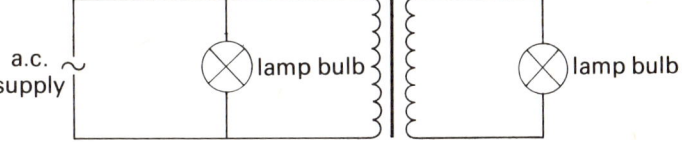

Is there any electrical connection between primary and secondary circuits? What does link the two circuits? You have, in effect, made a transformer from its basic parts. ▶ Does the transformer work on d.c.? If you are not sure, try it. ◀

Compare the current through the secondary lamp in this part with the current through the galvanometer in parts a, b and c. Suggest why this is of practical importance.

You will learn more about transformers in a later section. Figure 11.35 on page 74 shows some uses of transformers. See if you can find other uses. Describe the action of a transformer in terms of building blocks.

Part e

▷ ▶ Predict the effect of altering the number of turns on (a) the primary coil and (b) the secondary coil. Try it and see if you were correct. ◀

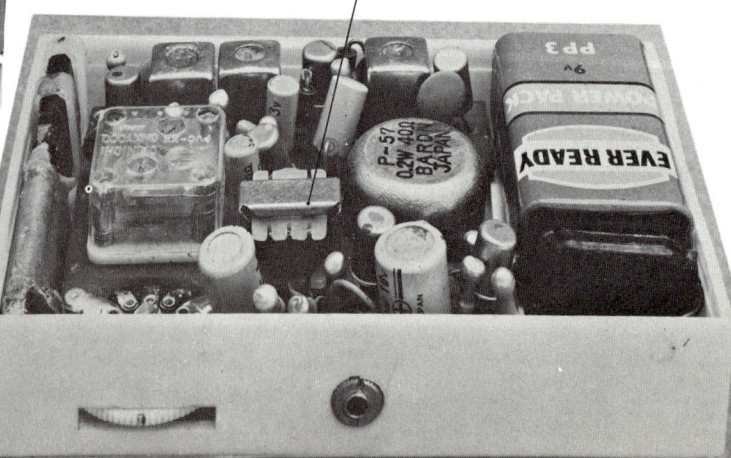

Figure 11.35a
A transformer

Figure 11.35b
An isolating transformer to
reduce the danger from electric
shock

Figure 11.35c
A transformer in a transistor
radio

transformer

Part f

▷ ▶ Predict and test the effect of an air-gap in the core. What is the simple pattern relating the magnetic field to the materials used? ◀

Give the pattern of electromagnetic induction in a form which covers all the investigations you have done.

Investigation 11.15 Electromagnetism and communication

Most indirect methods of communication these days are electrical. The commonest is the telephone: what are some of the others? In all of them information is carried electrically after being converted from the original form into electrical variations. The information may be stored (e.g. on tape) or transmitted over long distances using radio waves. Finally the information is turned back into the original form. (More details can be found in the *Patterns* topic books *Sound – its uses and misuses* and *Electromagnetic radiation*.)

Devices which convert information from one form to another are often referred to as transducers. A microphone is a transducer from sound to electricity. What name is given to a transducer from electricity to sound? Both of these can be electromagnetic devices (although there are other types as well).

Part a

▶ Figures 11.36 and 11.37 show a moving-coil microphone and a ribbon microphone. Use the pattern of electromagnetic induction to explain how in each case the rapid back-and-forth movement of the air which we call sound gives rise to a corresponding alternating current. ◀

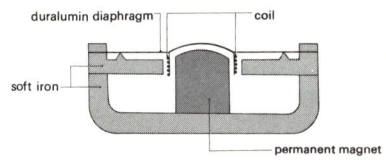

Figure 11.36
Moving-coil microphone

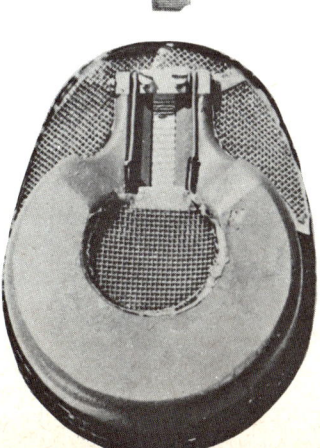

Figure 11.37
Ribbon microphone

67

Figure 11.38
Moving-coil loudspeaker

▶ A loudspeaker of the normal moving-coil sort is shown in figure 11.38. Use the patterns of electromagnetism to explain how the alternating currents in the coil produce sound waves. ◀

▶ In some communications systems (Figure 11.39) a small loudspeaker is used both for its normal purpose, and as a microphone as well. Explain how this is possible. ◀

Part b

Telecommunications is a rapidly growing industry in this country. Figure 11.40 shows how the number of telephones has grown in the past, and is expected to grow in the future. What is likely to cause the rate of growth to slacken eventually?

Figure 11.40

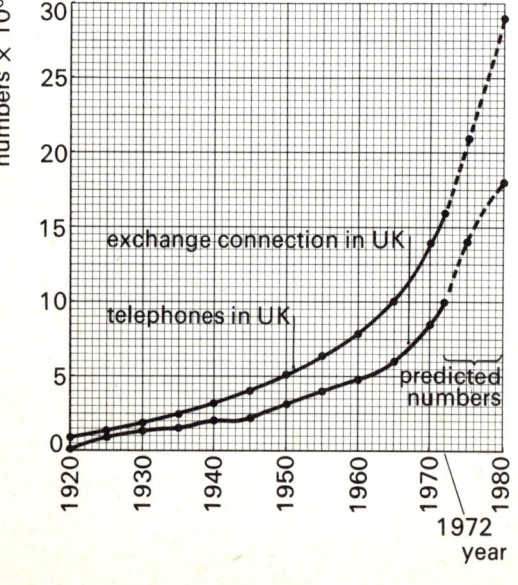

Telephone calls do not cost the same amount at different times of the day. The following table indicates the time (in seconds) bought in May, 1972 for 1p on calls dialled directly.

distance	peak rate Mon.–Fri. 9 a.m.–noon	standard rate Mon.–Fri. 8 a.m.–9 a.m. noon–6 p.m.	cheap rate 6 p.m.–8 a.m. and all day Sat. and Sun.
local	360 s	360 s	720 s
trunk calls			
Up to 56 km	20 s	30 s	72 s
56 to 80 km	12 s	15 s	36 s
Over 80 km	8 s	10 s	36 s

Figure 11.39
Intercom system

Figure 11.41 *left*
Electromagnectic switchgear
(Strowger system)

Figure 11.41 *right*
Electronic switchgear
(TXE 2 system)

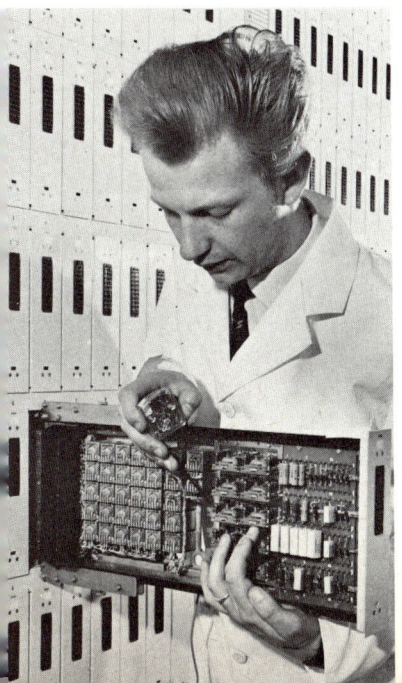

What can you deduce about the most popular time for people to use the telephone? Why is this the most popular time? What is the advantage in the sort of pricing system used?

In addition to the increasing number of telephones, people with telephones are tending to make more calls. What are the implications of this for the telephone exchanges throughout the country? At present nearly all the automatic exchanges in this country use switching equipments incorporating relays and electromagnetic selectors (which work on a similar principle), both of which depend on the patterns of this section. However there are several disadvantages to these electromagnet systems: they are bulky, relatively slow in operation and dissipate considerable amounts of energy. Modern electronic systems overcome all these, and in addition are more reliable. They do not depend on the electromagnetic patterns you have been using, and have no mechanical moving parts. Despite all these advantages, no fully electronic exchanges are being installed at present in this country, although 350 are being provided with partly electronic equipments (TXE2). The reasons are as follows.

In the late 1950s the Post Office considered whether it might replace the exchange system then in use (the Strowger system which dated from around 1912) by an electronic switching system. The transistor which could be used for switching had been invented in 1948 and its development was making rapid progress, so the idea seemed reasonable at the time. Several other countries took a more cautious line, and decided on a slightly more modern electromagnetic system called the crossbar-system. What arguments can you suggest for and against this caution?

In the event, the idea of moving towards a purely electronic switching system proved to have certain disadvantages. This new system took much longer to develop than had been expected, with the result that over 95 per cent of the equipment in use in Britain is still of the Strowger type. Countries which cautiously decided to adopt the crossbar system in the 1950s have been able to replace most or all of their Strowger equipment with crossbar, but in Britain this system was introduced only in 1966, so that the present provision is mostly Strowger, with some crossbar, and some TXE2.

Early in 1973 a major decision was taken. The choice was between the TXE4 (a partly electronic system similar to TXE2, but of greater capacity and improved design) which is now fully developed, and some more advanced, probably fully electronic system, which is not yet available. The latter alternative would have meant a very large investment in more crossbar equipment to bridge the gap between the old Strowger and the new system. In fact, the decision was made to introduce TXE4 as well as crossbar. Up to 1980 it is planned to spend £350 million on crossbar and £100 million on TXE4.

Discuss what factors had to be considered in making this decision. Bear in mind that there are only three major companies in the British telecommunications industry GEC/AEI, Plessey, and STC. Until 1969 there was an agreement by which most orders from the Post Office were divided between them on a percentage basis, 40 per cent for the first two firms and 20 per cent for STC. It is also relevant that GEC/AEI and Plessey both decided to make crossbar equipment in the 1960s, while STC began to develop TXE4.

Figure 11.42 illustrates the alternatives between which the choice was made.

Figure 11.42
Possible telephone systems
(simplified)

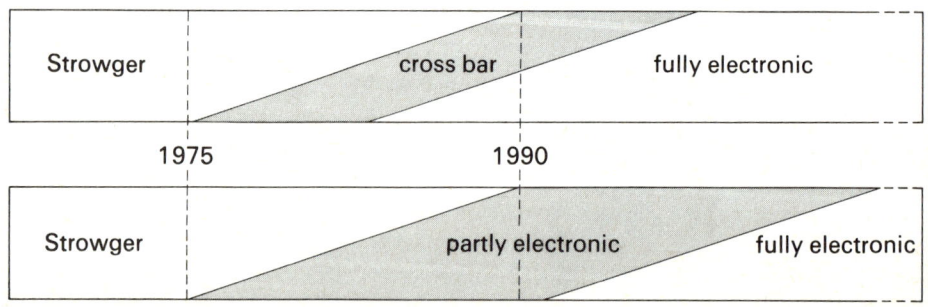

Part c

▷Increasingly other sorts of information which do not involve speech are being transmitted from place to place throughout the

Figure 11.43
A teleprinter

country and throughout the world. For many years the Telex system has been in worldwide use, mainly for business purposes. A circuit is set up between two teleprinters, so that whatever is typed on one is also typed automatically on the other. You may have seen a teleprinter, similar to the one shown in figure 11.43, being used to display the football results. Telex signals do not have to carry as much information as is required for intelligible speech, and this means that lines can be used more effectively. However, the lines can transmit information faster than anyone can type, so punched paper tape prepared in advance is often used for the input, and a similar tape for the output. The output tape can be fed through one of several teleprinters, so that the maximum capacity of the line can be used. What are the advantages of Telex over the telephone?

Figure 11.44
The Telex code. What is the message on the tape?

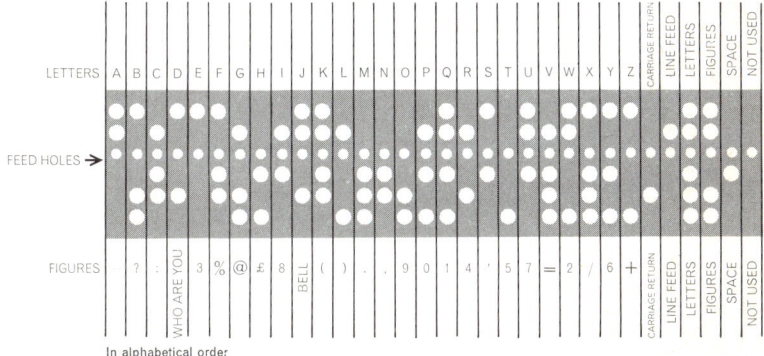

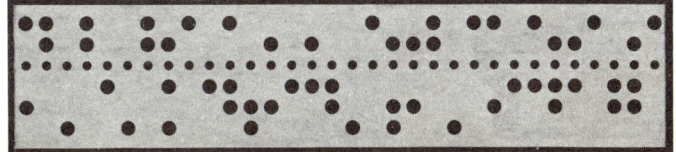

▶A teleprinter depends on the electromagnetic pattern of this section. Suggest in general terms how it might work. ◀

Most of the business messages sent by Telex consist of words, with some numerical data. An increasing number of 'data terminals' are coming into use, by which computers can be used by people at a considerable distance. The user has input and output devices, which in the simplest case consist of a single teleprinter very similar to the Telex one, but can include instruments working with paper tape, computer cards and magnetic tape, line printers, graph plotters and cathode-ray-tube displays (see figure 11.45). Information is fed to and from the central computer by many users along either Telex or telephone lines, or by means of private lines.

Capacity of different types of circuit

system	capacity/binary digits per second
Telex	50
Datel 100 (on telex network)	50
Datel 100 (on private telegraph circuit)	110
Datel 200	200
Datel 600 (on public telephone network)	600
Datel 600 (on private circuit)	1 200
Datel 2 400	2 400
Datel 48K (wide-band private circuit, equivalent to 12 telephone channels	48 000

Figure 11.45a
Card reader

Figure 11.45c
Magnetic display unit

Figure 11.45b
Graphical display unit

At present the UK has about 20 000 data terminals, more than the rest of Europe together. Only the US has more. Some of the main users are banks, airlines, universities and major industrial firms. Suggest reasons why rapid access to a computer from a distance might be important for each of these.

All the above depend on a circuit being set up in advance, and maintained throughout the message. This is called line-switching. However, a new method of dealing with messages is being introduced which works in a quite different way. This is called message-switching, and is in some ways more like delivering a letter. Each message has its destination included, like the address on an envelope. The message is sent along the network from one point to another under the control of central computers. At each point of its journey the message can be sent by alternative routes. If one route is damaged or busy another is selected. Finally the message reaches its destination. Long messages may be broken up and sent separately, possibly by different routes. An essential part of the system is the ability to store each message for a time at each switching centre, until the next section of its route is decided. Suggest reasons why message-switching is increasingly being preferred for the transfer of data. What would be essential if this system were to be used for speech-communication, e.g. telephones?

New developments in communications are under way. It is possible now to purchase a device which will produce a copy of any document at a distance, using an ordinary telephone line. 'Viewphones' are in use experimentally, and will probably come into use as soon as adequate capacity for sending information is available. (A viewphone needs the equivalent of 200 telephone lines.)

Figure 11.46
a Rank Xerox 400 telecopier facsimile transceiver

b Viewphone

Discuss the effect of the changes mentioned above on the lives of people during the next twenty (or more) years. How important is communication and information-transfer?

12 Earth, water and organism interactions

Until very recently man, along with all other living things, has been more or less confined to an interface between two very different states of matter – the Earth and its atmosphere. Although the surface of the Earth is a very small part of the whole Universe, it is very important because it plays such a large part in our lives. You will remember comparing the surface of the Moon, which has no atmosphere, with that of the Earth, which has one. It would be quite justifiable to suggest that the great differences between the two are due to the many interactions which take place on the Earth between its surface, the organisms which inhabit it and the atmosphere.

In recent sections you have studied interactions between building blocks of the same type: between populations, or between particles, for example. In this section you will be investigating interactions between different types of building block, both large and small. These interactions can be very complicated and difficult to 'unravel'.

At the surface of much of the Earth that is dry land there is a thin layer of soil. The very existence of man and other organisms depends on this soil layer as the direct result of many interactions. Discuss those which are familiar to you.

Investigation 12.1 What is soil?

You will need

microscope and microslide
soil samples
soil auger
gas jar or large measuring cylinder

Examine a little soil, thinly spread on a microslide, with the microscope. Two-thirds fill a gas jar with water. Add soil until the water nearly reaches the top. Place your hand firmly over the open end and shake vigorously. Allow to settle. Describe the appearance of the settled soil. The table on page 76 shows the sizes of different types of soil particle.

particle	diameter/mm
stones	above 2
coarse sand	2–0.2
fine sand	0.2–0.02
silt	0.02–0.002
clay	below 0.0002

    If possible dig a trench similar to the one shown in figure 12.1, opposite. If not use the soil auger to remove soil samples every 10 cm from a bore-hole. Compare your soil profile with those in figure 12.1. What pattern is observable in the sizes of the rocks at different depths? Collect selected stones or rocks from different depths. Note the depth and store them for future identification (in Section 14). ▶From the pattern of rock size in profiles suggest the origin of soil. ◀

Investigation 12.2   Interactions between man and the soil

Figure 12.2a–c
Landscape patterns:

You will need

land capability map

a Chalk soil landscape

b Sandy soil landscape

Figure 12.1
Soil profiles

The Soil Survey of England and Wales is an organisation concerned to find out about soils, to map them and discover their properties and characteristics. The knowledge they gain should help in a number of ways, particularly with decisions about which land should be retained for agriculture or which could best be used for building and other purposes. One of their activities is to produce land capability maps to provide a guide in planning the best use of land. Examine one of these maps. What factors interact to determine patterns of land capability?

Throughout history man has become so integrated with the soil that much of our landscape reflects this interaction (see figure 12.2). Broadly speaking there are four different types of soil found in Great Britain: sandy soils, clayey soils, loamy soils and chalky soils.

soil type	coarse and fine sand/%	clay/%	silt/%
sandy soil	> 70	< 20	—
loam	70–40	20–40	—
clay soil	30–40	30–40	30–40

The table shows some of the characteristics of three of these. Chalky soils are fairly similar to loamy soils in composition but often of

c Loamy soil landscape

a Dairy farming is common on clay soils

b Sandy loams are useful for market gardening

c Peat soils in Lincolnshire are used extensively for bulb growing

lighter colour and usually contain small pieces of chalk rock. Peaty soils contain large quantities of humus. Loamy soils range from heavy loams (with a large amount of clay) to sandy loams (with a much higher proportion of sand). With the help of a local Ordnance Survey map you can begin a soil survey of your district. Whenever you collect a sample (as on a field trip) make a note of:

a where collected (pinpoint on the map)
b the use to which the land is (or is not) put
c any evidence of the underlying rock from which the soil may be derived.

You can make a soil analysis by examining with a microscope and shaking with water as before in order to identify the soil type from the table on page 76.

As you move about your district (and even a much wider area) consider how man's interaction with the soil reflects what you see (see figure 12.3). Look, for instance, for patterns of agriculture or horticulture. Look for patterns of interaction between soil and plant communities. How do place names reflect soil types? You could enter details and photographs in a logbook kept at school which would build up into a very useful record.

d Forest plantations on sandy soil

Figure 12.3
Interactions of man and the soil

Investigation 12.3 The origin of soil

Figure 12.4 *left*
Interactions involved in soil formation:
Frost weathered rock: on the left large rocks shattered from the rock face can be seen. In the foreground plants can be seen colonising rocks and rock crevices. What interactions are illustrated by this picture?

Figure 12.4 *right*
Plants colonising sand-dunes. What interaction involved in soil formation is illustrated?

From the evidence seen in Investigation 12.1 it would appear that soil originates from the underlying rock. How? What are the processes involved?

You will need

access to oven, refrigerator and water supply

fragments of rock specimens

crucibles

dilute hydrochloric acid

Discuss the interactions between various building blocks (and sometimes non-building blocks) which may be involved in the formation of soil from rocks. (The list of apparatus above may help. Why is an acid included?) Devise ways of testing your suggestions. Contrast these laboratory experiments with real conditions. Discuss the part played by organisms in soil formation.

Investigation 12.4 Weathering of buildings

The photographs shown in figure 12.5a–b show the effects of weathering on St. Paul's cathedral. Is this likely to occur with modern structural material? Should the maintenance of buildings such as St. Paul's be a national responsibility?

Figure 12.5a
Weathering of stone used for building

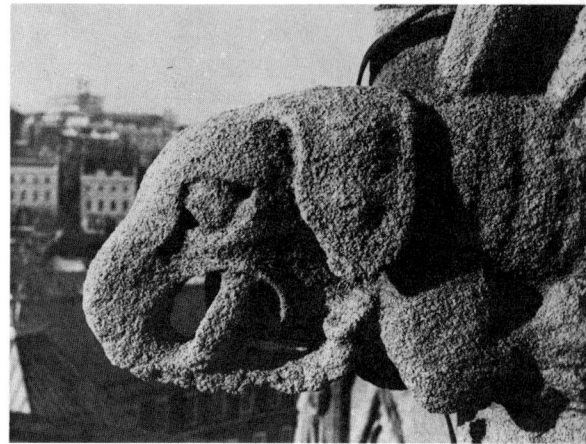

Figure 12.5b
Weathering on stone sculpture

Figures 12.5c–d show how man has interacted with the Earth in building design.

Figure 12.5c
Flat roofs in a Greek village evolved to collect scanty rainfall, the only source of water. The channel which transfers rain water to a storage tank can be seen on the house, lower centre left

Figure 12.5d
The Hotel Intercontinental in Managua, Nicaragua, designed to withstand earthquake damage. It was one of the few buildings to survive the recent earthquake

You have already investigated the effects on the rate of particle interaction of introducing a catalyst. Solid size and solution concentration are two other factors also worth considering, particularly as both of these could affect weathering of rock and structural materials.

Investigation 12.5 Porosity

You will need

microscope (or hand lens) and watch glass
pieces of marble and limestone
dropper pipette
access to a balance

Examine pieces of marble and limestone. Examine the surfaces under a microscope (using a lamp to illuminate from the top and side) or a hand lens. Devise experiments to determine whether the pieces absorb water, and then carry out these experiments after discussion with your teacher. In what way do your observations contribute to an understanding of the results obtained from experiments in Investigation 12.3?

Investigation 12.6 Solid size and rate of reaction

This is a demonstration experiment. You will be finding the rate of the reaction between marble and hydrochloric acid for different sizes of marble. Link the results of the experiment with your observations in previous investigations.

Investigation 12.7 Concentration and rate of reaction

▶Devise an experiment (similar to the previous investigation) to discover what effect different concentrations of acid have on the rate of the reaction between marble and hydrochloric acid. ◀ The actual experiment will be demonstrated.

In industrial areas the rain is sometimes more acidic than normal. Why? How would this affect the weathering of buildings in such areas?

You will need

conical flask, 100 cm³
measuring cylinder, 25 cm³
beaker, 100 cm³
stop clock or watch with seconds hand
2.0M hydrochloric acid
sodium thiosulphate solution
clean white paper

The reaction between sodium thiosulphate and hydrochloric acid is:

$$Na_2S_2O_3(aq) + 2HCl(aq) \rightarrow$$
$$H_2O(l) + SO_2(g) + 2NaCl(aq) + S(s).$$

Measure out 50 cm³ of sodium thiosulphate solution into the conical flask. Add 5 cm³ of the acid to the flask, and start the clock. Swirl the mixture and place the flask on a piece of white paper with a cross drawn on it. Look vertically down through the solution and note the time taken for the cross to disappear.

Repeat the experiment using 10, 20, 30 and 40 cm³ of sodium thiosulphate solution made up in each case to 50 cm³ with water. Plot a graph of original volume of sodium thiosulphate solution taken against time. What effect has concentration of sodium thiosulphate on the rate of reaction? If time permits, you could find the effect on rate of varying the acid concentration.

Investigation 12.9 An explanation

▶Give an explanation for the results of the experiments in the above investigations based on your understanding of the kinetic theory. ◀

You have seen that soil affects the type of landscape in a particular area. However, much of this landscape is artificial in the sense that it is the result of an interaction with man. It is probably obvious to you that the underlying rocks will also play a large part in forming the basic framework of the landscape within which man and other organisms interact. This gives rise to many questions, simple to ask, but more difficult to answer. For example, how do mountains arise? Why does one part of the country have an underlying bedrock of chalk, whereas another part, perhaps much less than one kilometre

Figure 12.6

away, has an underlying bedrock of sandstone? Many such questions can be posed as the result of noticing patterns in the Earth's crust. They are important because they affect people's lives. The whole economy of a district frequently depends on the underlying rocks. Figure 12.6 shows one example. Suggest others.

Investigation 12.10 Looking for patterns in the Earth's crust

N.B. – At about this time you may be going on a field trip or trips. You will be given a planned programme which will suit your own area. Some of the work you will be able to perform on a field trip will be connected with investigations in this section. Sometimes, as in this investigation, the work you do could replace that in this manual.

The photographs in figures 12.7–12.15 on pages 84 and 85 illustrate some earth patterns. Have you seen similar patterns in your locality? If you are able to see those patterns on a field trip collect specimens of the different rock strata. Label each specimen and sketch indicating exactly where each specimen was collected. In Section 14 you will have a chance to identify them.

Figure 12.7
A stratified rock pattern

Figure 12.8
A fault in the stratification

Figure 12.11
Folded strata lying on horizontal strata

Figure 12.12
Horizontal strata lying on nearly vertical strata

Figure
12.14
A pattern
in strata
known as
cross-
bedding

Figure 12.9
al stratifications

Figure 12.13
A close-up view showing
gradation in the size of the rock
particles in strata

Figure 12.10a and b
This folded pattern is known as an anticline (the upfold) and the syncline
(the downfold)

Figure 12.15
Examples in which the upper
strata bulge down into the lower
strata can sometimes be found

How have these patterns of structure in the Earth's crust arisen?
What processes have been involved? What interactions are responsible? You have seen that rock is slowly weathered into smaller and
smaller particles in a variety of interactions in which water is often
involved. The interactions between water and the Earth also play
a large part in determining the patterns in the Earth's crust. Sometimes the interactions are on a massive and catastrophic scale, as the
next investigation shows.

Investigation 12.11 The Lynmouth flood

A disastrous flood occurred during the night of 15/16 August, 1952, in North Devon, at and around the seaside town of Lynmouth. The rain gauge on Longstone Barrow, Exmoor, the tableland above Lynmouth, recorded 9.1 inches (232 mm) of rain during the 14 hours. Such rainfall has been exceeded only four times since official records began in Britain 100 years ago. Remember that ordinary steady rain for 24 hours means less than 1 inch (25 mm) in a rain gauge. . . . In one or more areas rainfall probably exceeded 9.1 inches (232 mm); . . . the heaviest local fall was about 4 inches (100 mm) in an hour.

The state of the ground made conditions worse. It was already waterlogged, and just below the surface a layer of rock prevented any appreciable percolation of water. Moreover, the East and West Lyn Rivers, and their tributaries, fall 1 500 feet (455 mm) through funnel-like gorges into Lynmouth in under 4 miles (6.4 km). Down these gorges on that terrible night pounded millions of tons of flood water. In dry summer weather the rivers have a depth of a few inches; now, at times, a solid wall of water up to 40 feet (12 m) high raced down to the sea at 20 mph (32 km per hour).

Such a torrent is irresistible to everything except the heaviest and most solidly based objects. The water gouged out huge rocks and boulders – some weighing 15 tonnes (1.5×10^4 kg) – and carried them to the seashore. Telegraph poles and motor-cars followed. Trees felled by earlier gales, and others washed out by the roots, were swept into the sea. The next morning, half a mile out to sea, hundreds of trees, presumably weighted down by rocks and soil entangled in their enormous roots, had their upper branches showing above the waves – a fantastic sea forest of stunted trees.

The flood waters dug deep into the Earth. Road surfaces were scoured away, and the soft soil of the verges was gouged as by a giant excavator, some gullies being 20 feet (6 m) deep – right down to the bare rock. The Lynmouth sewerage system and two-thirds of the water mains were ruined. A vivid illustration of this gouging effect of the flood occurred at a Lynmouth garage. Here petrol tanks were scoured from their foundations and swept away without a trace.

When dawn broke the scene on the foreshore was fantastic. It was littered with the debris of scores of wrecked homes and buildings; smashed cars; telegraph poles, tree trunks, branches and complete trees; and smashed and mangled remains of the

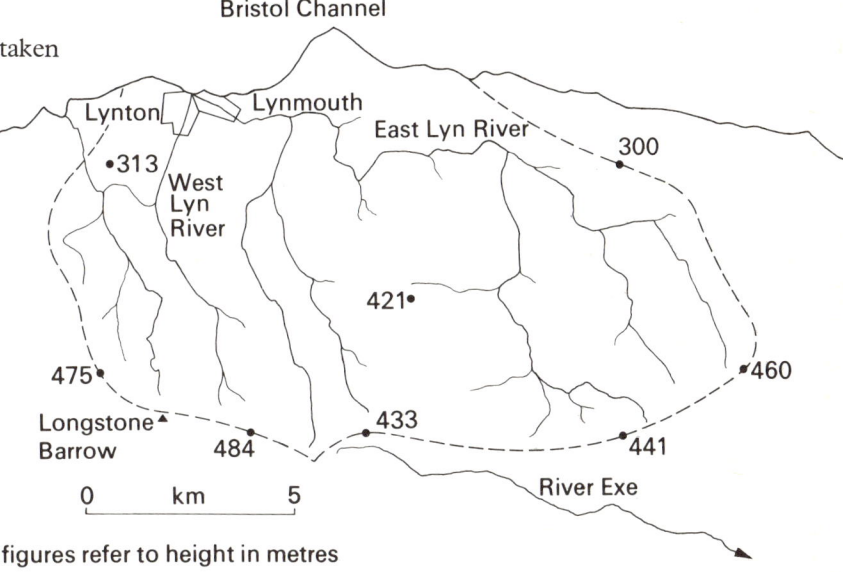

Figure 12.16
Aerial view of Lynmouth taken
on 17th August 1952

Figure 12.17
A map showing the area
around Lynmouth

undergrowth from the surrounding countryside; some 200 000 cubic yards (150 000 m³) of silt, mud, gravel and stones, in some places massed 25 feet (7.5 m) high; some 40 000 tons (4×70^7 kg) of rocks and boulders; iron girders and bridges; broken masonry and the bodies of fish, birds, animals – and people

Make a list of the interacting factors involved in this disaster. Draw a diagram showing the stream gradient, the rainfall totals and build-up of water towards the sea, and the rock and soil debris moved to form the foreshore deposit. Include the words 'erosion', 'transport of debris' and 'deposition' in your labels.

Investigation 12.12 Insuring against disaster

Read the following extract:

'Sorry there is no return envelope,' wrote Linda Sage when she sent this report. 'Our post office has been blown away.'

At about 4 a.m. Martin and I woke up with the feeling that something was wrong. 'Let's see where the hurricane is,' he suggested, so we got out our tracking chart and turned on the radio. Sure enough, the capricious Celia had changed course. When we had gone to bed, she was heading for Houston, about two hundred miles up the coast. Now she was making a beeline for our backyard.

'Let's go!' I decided, scooping up a suitcase with one hand and plucking our baby out of his cot with the other. Martin took one last look at his new hi-fi equipment and I gazed fondly on our Conran curtains. Then we were charging through the night in our tiny Volkswagen, our baby asleep in the back and our cat curled up on the floor. Even now lightning was on every horizon and the wind was doing some preliminary exercises. Oh, to be back in England. . . .

Fifty miles inland we came across a small town on fairly high ground, which seemed a good place to ride out the storm. The rest of the day we sat in the safety of a motel room, with our ears glued to the radio as the hurricane spun its way to the central Texas coast. At 3 p.m. it struck land at Port Aransas and Aransas Pass, one the site of Martin's laboratory and the other of our home. Were we to be made jobless and homeless at the same time?

During the hurricane, residents who had been too stubborn to leave their houses were blasted with winds of 160 m.p.h. from the south-east. Then came the eye, bringing uncanny calm and time to look out at the chaos all around. Then the wind started up from the other direction, this time doing even more damage than before.

Shortly after the storm began, the radio and television stations from the Corpus Christi area were all silenced. 'The whole building is shaking, huge pieces of metal are flying around outside, the street is being lacerated by a hail of fine glass from broken windows, palm trees are bending into a U-shape . . .' and then we heard no more. The television studio itself had been wrecked.

Soon all the telephone lines were dead too. The hurricane area was completely cut off from the outside world. Later that night, the small hospital in our home town managed to get out a message. Only its shell was left and it was housing hurricane victims urgently in need of blood, splints, and medicines. Could anyone help?

When light broke the next day, the vast extent of the damage became visible. Corpus Christi, a city of 200,000, had few windows intact. The neighbouring towns of Rockport, Gregory, and Portland were badly damaged. Ingleside was on fire from three huge oil storage tanks ignited by sparks from flying metal or lightning. But our home town, Aransas Pass, was worst hit of all. When we heard that 90 per cent of the buildings (most of which were made of wood, not brick) had been destroyed, we resigned ourselves, the longer we took, the longer we could hope. Part of the low-lying road had been washed away but we managed to negotiate it. As we neared home, the road was littered with torn down cables, poles, rotting vegetation, and, at one point, a whole house which had been lifted up by the wind and deposited half way across the road. The fields, which stretch as far as the eye can see, had been laden with maize and cotton,

ready for harvesting. Now the plants were bowed down on the ground, acknowledging an awesome force which had just passed their way.

Our hearts sank as we turned the corner of our road. But there was our house, four walls and a roof, all intact. But the sturdy, old oak trees surrounding it had been snapped in two like matchsticks and it was no longer surrounded by a fence. Hoof marks in the front garden told of stampeding cows seeking refuge from the storm. And the whole area looked as if winter had suddenly come – there was not a single leaf left on any of the trees.

Looking around now, we realise how lucky we were. We are surrounded by houses whose roofs have been snatched by the hurricane, piles of rubble that were once homes, mobile homes that were tossed-up in the air and flung down again upside down, their bellies split open and their innards spilling out.

Cars are buried under piles of rubble, lorries are wrapped round trees, street signs scattered like confetti, and porches peeled off. Glass, metal, trees, dustbins clutter the streets. Shrimp boats are herded together in the harbour like sardines. Smaller boats look as if they were made of balsa wood. Silos resemble crushed aluminium tubes. Over the whole town hangs black, oily smoke and a smell of rotting debris. Last week there was a town here. Now there is a pile of refuse.

Like us, the rest of the town is back to pick up the pieces. A man stands in the remains of his house. 'That used to be the kitchen,' he says. A woman delves into the deep pile of objects heaped on the flattened walls of her house. She picks out a blouse and hangs it on a tree, smoothing out the folds. A family sits around its dining table, eating a midday meal from a tin, but they have no walls around them. Everywhere is the sound of sawing, hammering, screwing.

Our grocer waves and smiles from what used to be his shop. He wades his way out through crushed tins and broken glass. 'Guess I won't be open today.'

GENERAL ACCIDENT FIRE & LIFE ASSURANCE CORPORATION LTD

HEAD OFFICE
GENERAL BUILDINGS, PERTH, SCOTLAND

Section 1   THE BUILDINGS

The Property Insured

The Insured's house situate at the address stated in the Schedule and which is Brick, Stone or Concrete built with Slate, Tile, Asphalt, Metal or Concrete roof except as specially mentioned and all the Garages and Outbuildings on the same premises and used in connection therewith including Landlord's Fixtures and Fittings therein or thereon and the walls, gates and fences around and pertaining thereto.

Extension

The insurance on the buildings includes:

(i) Architects', Surveyors', Legal and other Fees (not exceeding those authorised under the scales of the various Institutions and/or Bodies regulating such charges) necessarily incurred in connection with the reinstatement of the property insured consequent upon its destruction or damage but not such Fees for preparing a claim or estimate of loss.

(ii) Expenses necessarily incurred by the Insured with the consent of the Corporation in:
  (a) removing debris
  (b) dismantling and/or demolishing
  (c) shoring-up or propping
of the property insured consequent upon its destruction or damage.

(iii) The cost of complying with building or other regulations under or framed in pursuance of any Act of Parliament or with Bye-Laws of any Municipal or Local Authority (but not where notice has been served upon the Insured prior to the happening of the loss destruction or damage) but only in so far as these relate to the damaged portions of the property.

The Corporation's liability under the above extension and for loss or damage by any of the contingencies insured shall not exceed in the aggregate the sum insured on the buildings.

Contingencies relating to Buildings

Loss or damage caused by:

A 1 Fire, Lightning, Earthquake and Explosion.

2 Riot, Civil Commotion, Labour Disturbances and Malicious Persons but excluding all such loss or damage in the Republic of Ireland and Northern Ireland.

3 Aircraft and other Aerial devices or articles dropped therefrom.

4 Theft or any attempt thereat excluding cover during any period in excess of 30 days when the house is left insufficiently furnished for full habitation.

5 Leakage of Fuel from any fixed oil-fired heating installation.

6 Bursting or Overflowing of Water Tanks, Apparatus or Pipes excluding:
  (i) the first £15 of each and every loss
  (ii) destruction or damage caused during any period in excess of 30 days when the house is left insufficiently furnished for full habitation.

7 Storm and Flood excluding:
  (i) Destruction or damage caused by Frost

(ii) Destruction or damage caused by Subsidence or Landslip

(iii) Destruction or damage to Fences, Gates and Earth Retaining Walls

(iv) The first £15 of each and every loss.

8 Subsidence or Landslip of the site on which the buildings stand but excluding in respect of each and every claim the first £150 or 3% of the sum insured, whichever is the greater.

9 Impact by any vehicle or animal provided that the Corporation shall not be responsible for the first £15 of such damage if caused by a vehicle or animal belonging to or under the control of the Insured or any person residing with him.

10 Breakage of Receiving Aerials, Aerial Fittings and Masts (excluding damage caused thereto).

The Corporation further will indemnify the Insured in respect of:

B   LOSS OF RENT
  (i) Loss of Rent by the Insured as owner
  (ii) Loss of Ground Rent for up to two years
  (iii) Reasonable Additional Cost of alternative accommodation necessarily incurred

if the buildings are so damaged by any of the contingencies specified in Section A as to be rendered uninhabitable, but only in respect of the period necessary for re-instatement for a total amount not exceeding 10% of the sum insured on the buildings.

C   DAMAGE TO UNDERGROUND PIPES AND CABLES. Accidental damage to underground water, drain, sewage and gas pipes and underground electricity, telephone and television cables extending from the buildings to the public mains, and underground fuel oil pipes.

D   BREAKAGE OF FIXED GLASS AND WASHBASINS. Breakage of fixed glass, washbasins, sinks, baths, lavatory pans and cisterns. The cover by this section is inoperative when the house is not sufficiently furnished for full habitation.

E   PROPERTY OWNER'S LIABILITY. Liability of the Insured as owner and not as occupier of the buildings in respect of accidents happening during the period of insurance in or about the buildings resulting in:

1 bodily injury to any person not in the employment of the Insured

2 damage to property not belonging to or in the charge of or under the control of the Insured or a member of his family or household or a person in his employment.

Provided always that the amount payable hereunder in respect of any one accident or series of accidents constituting one occurrence shall not exceed the sum of £100,000 in addition to Claimant's costs and expenses, and Insured's costs and expenses incurred with the consent of the Corporation.

Claims are excluded in respect of:

(i) injury or damage arising out of:
  (a) the Insured's profession or business
  (b) the use of lifts or vehicles

(ii) liability arising out of any contract which imposes upon the Insured liability which the Insured would not otherwise have been under.

GENERAL EXCEPTIONS

This Policy does not cover:

(a) any contingency—

    (1) occasioned by or happening through War, Invasion, Act of Foreign Enemy, Hostilities (whether war be declared or not), Civil War, Rebellion, Revolution, Insurrection or Military or Usurped Power.

    (2) In the Republic of Ireland and Northern Ireland — occasioned by or happening through Riot or Civil Commotion.

(b) (1) loss or destruction of or damage to any property whatsoever or any loss or expense whatsoever resulting or arising therefrom or any consequential loss

    (2) any legal liability of whatsoever nature

directly or indirectly caused by or contributed to by or arising from:

    (i) ionising radiations or contamination by radioactivity from any nuclear fuel or from any nuclear waste from the combustion of nuclear fuel.

    (ii) the radioactive, toxic, explosive or other hazardous properties of any explosive nuclear assembly or nuclear component thereof.

(c) loss, destruction or damage directly occasioned by pressure waves caused by aircraft and other aerial devices travelling at sonic or supersonic speeds.

GENERAL CONDITIONS

1 If at the time of any loss, damage, or liability arising under this policy there shall be any other insurance, whether effected by the Insured or by any other person or persons acting on his behalf, covering such loss, damage or liability or any part thereof, the Corporation shall not be liable for more than its rateable proportion thereof.

2 The Insured shall on the happening of any loss, damage or accident give immediate notice thereof in writing to the Corporation with such detailed particulars as may be reasonably required. In the case of loss or damage by Burglary, House-breaking, Robbery or Theft or any attempt thereat he shall also immediately notify the Police.

3 The Insured shall send to the Corporation immediately any writ, summons or other legal process and shall give all necessary information and assistance to enable the Corporation to negotiate the claim or to institute proceedings and the Insured shall not negotiate, pay, settle, admit or repudiate any claim without the written consent of the Corporation.

4 The Corporation shall be entitled:

    (a) On the happening of any loss or damage to enter any building where the loss or damage has happened and to take and keep possession of the property and to deal with the salvage in a reasonable manner. No property may be abandoned to the Corporation.

    (b) To undertake in the name and on the behalf of the Insured the absolute conduct control and settlement of any proceedings and to take proceedings at its own expense and for its own benefit but in the name of the Insured, to recover compensation or secure indemnity from any third party in respect of anything covered by this policy.

5 If any claim under this policy shall be in any respect fraudulent or if any fraudulent means or devices are used by the Insured or anyone acting on his behalf to obtain any benefit under this policy all benefit hereunder shall be forfeited.

6 If any difference shall arise as to the amount to be paid under this policy (liability being otherwise admitted) such difference shall be referred to an Arbitrator to be appointed by the parties in accordance with the Statutory Provisions in that behalf for the time being in force. Where any difference is by this Condition to be referred to arbitration the making of an award shall be a condition precedent to any right of action against the Corporation.

7 The sums insured are declared by the Insured to represent not less than the full value of the property insured and the total liability of the Corporation by all or any of the insured contingencies during any one period of insurance shall not exceed the sum insured against each item respectively or in the aggregate the total sum insured hereby or such other sum or sums as may be substituted therefor by endorsement hereon or attached hereto signed by or on behalf of the Corporation.

The Insured having made to the Corporation a written proposal and declaration which shall be the basis of this contract and having paid to the Corporation the premium,

The Corporation will indemnify the Insured in respect of the contingencies stated in the policy occurring during the period of insurance subject to the terms, exceptions and conditions contained herein or endorsed hereon.

For and on behalf of the Corporation

Chief General Manager

How would you react to having to live in a hurricane zone? It is possible to insure against some natural disasters.

Figure 12.18
Hurricane damage

Exactly what is, and what is not, insured by the policy on previous page? For what sort of risks do you think it wise to take out insurance policies? Is it worthwhile?

▷**Investigation 12.13 River action: an interaction between the Earth and water**

The Lynmouth flood demonstrated the effectiveness of river action over a short period of time. In this investigation you will attempt to assess the effect of more normal river activity.

You will need

apparatus for collecting samples of river water
large beaker
access to a balance
Bunsen burner, tripod, gauze and evaporating basin
hardboard mat
Ordnance Survey map(s) of the area drained by the river you examine

Collect or examine samples of river water (this is best done on a field excursion). Note the volume. For each sample collected, let any sediment (small soil particles) settle out. Pour off the water, allow the sediment to dry and measure its mass. The sediment you have measured is that which was being carried in suspension.
    Take a smaller sample of the remaining water, and evaporate it to obtain a measurement of the amount of material in solution. How much material is being transported per unit volume of river water? If you know the cross-sectional area of the river and its speed of flow when the sample was taken, calculate the amount of

Figure 12.19
Ice is also an important factor in weathering and eroding the Earth's crust. Glaciers flowing down mountain sides transport rock debris depositing it at the lower margins. As glaciers melt at their lower end finely ground rock is washed out and deposited

Figure 12.20
The mixture of soil and rock debris deposited by a glacier on melting. North of the Thames, many parts of Britain are covered by such debris deposited by retreating glaciers at the end of the last ice age.

material transported by the entire river in kilogrammes per second. Calculate the area of the river basin above the point from which the samples were taken. (Use the 1 km grid squares on the Ordnance Survey maps.) Calculate the quantity of rock and soil debris eroded from this area in:

a 1 year
b 1 000 years
c 1 million years.

What happens to all the sediment and debris transported by water?

Investigation 12.14 Investigating erosion, transportation and sedimentation

A number of laboratory experiments and demonstrations will be available for you to investigate in closer detail some of the processes involved in the erosion, transport and deposition of sediments. You will probably have an opportunity to investigate some of these processes in the field. Discuss the interacting factors involved.

Figure 12.21
Coastal erosion

Figure 12.22
Delta formation

 Record the nature of the deposits produced by the different pro-
cesses used in the experiments. Devise a cyclic flow chart, showing
the pattern of events in weathering, erosion of rock and soil, transport and sedimentation, rock formation, folding and movement.

Investigation 12.15 Explaining Earth patterns

►Explain each of the Earth patterns discussed in Investigation
12.14 indicating, if possible, the relative age of the strata. ◄

Investigation 12.16 Landscapes

You will need

rock specimens if available

In this investigation you need study only one of the given examples (or you may have an entirely different example suggested). Each figure shows (a) a photograph of the landscape and (b) the underlying rocks (of which you may be given specimens to examine.) ▶Explain the landscapes in terms of the history of the underlying patterns in the Earth's crust. ◀

Figure 12.23
Bratton Down, Wiltshire
a Landscape
b Underlying rock pattern

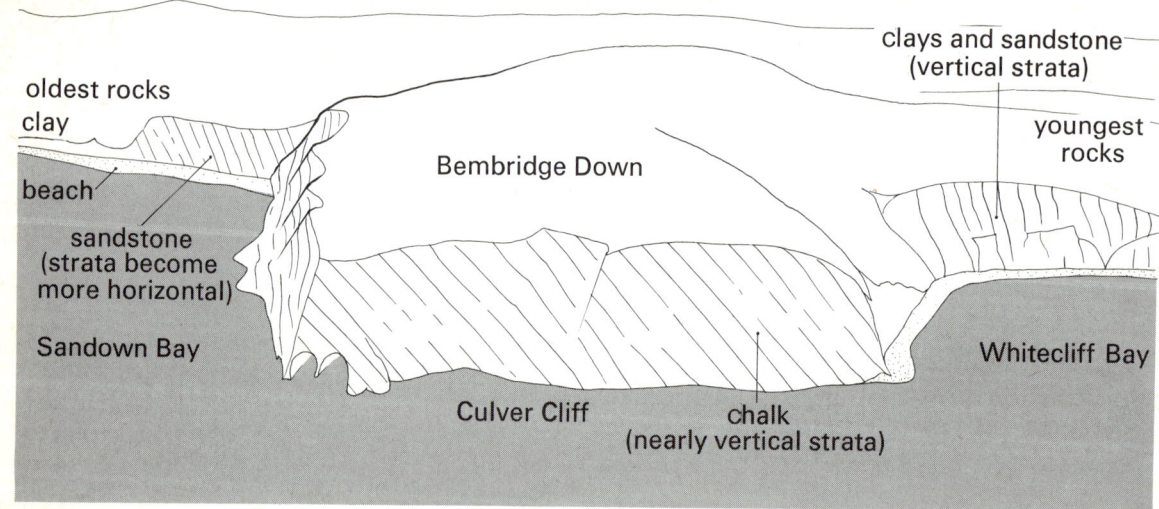

Figure 12.24
Bembridge Down and Culver
Cliff, Sandown, Isle of Wight
a Landscape
b Underlying rock pattern

13 Motion

Motion can be a feature of all building blocks regardless of size. Every day you meet situations in which movement is important. The photographs in figure 13.1 show some moving objects which you do not see every day. How do we describe motion? How can we measure motion? Is it possible to combine several motions? What practical problems are there connected with motion? These are some of the questions which this section will try to answer.

Figure 13.1
b Tracks of fast-moving charged particles in a magnetic field (bubble chamber photograph)

a Racing cars move at incredible speeds

c Supertankers are so large that walking would take too long

Investigation 13.1 Maps and vectors

Part a

You will need

Ordnance Survey map

You may have learned about vectors in mathematics. If not, there is an Appendix (see p. 151) to this book which will help you to understand the idea, which is summarised here.

A vector is a set of numbers in order. The simplest example is an ordered pair of numbers, written:

(12, 5)   row vector

or $\begin{pmatrix} 12 \\ 5 \end{pmatrix}$ column vector.

The separate numbers are called components.

An essential feature of vectors is that to add two vectors you add the separate components. For example:

$$\begin{pmatrix} 12 \\ 5 \end{pmatrix} + \begin{pmatrix} -2 \\ 4 \end{pmatrix} = \begin{pmatrix} 10 \\ 9 \end{pmatrix}$$

One component is unaffected by the other.

Vectors can represent many different things. There is always some difference between the factors represented by the different components. Some of the things which can be represented in this way are measurable quantities important in science.

On a map the distance eastward and the distance northward can be represented by the two components of a vector. On the map you are using find these two components for a journey of your choice (for example, from a road bridge over a stream to a church with a spire). Now find the components for a second journey starting from where the first one ended (for example, from the church to a railway station). Finally find the components for the combined journey (bridge to station).

Can these journeys be represented by vectors? To answer this question you need to see whether the components of the combined journey equal the numbers you obtain by adding the components for the separate journeys. Do they?

The 'official' name for journeys of this sort is displacements. Are displacements concerned with the route taken from one point to another? Any quantity which can be represented by a vector is called a vector quantity. Displacement is the simplest of these.

What is the pattern which must be true of any quantity which is a vector quantity?

What is the relationship between the displacement (1.2 km east and 0.5 km north) and the vector $\begin{pmatrix} 12 \\ 5 \end{pmatrix}$? The diagram (see figure 13.2) shows the displacement and its components as lines. Are these lines 1.2 km and 0.5 km long? What is the relationship between the lines on the paper and the actual displacement?

Figure 13.2

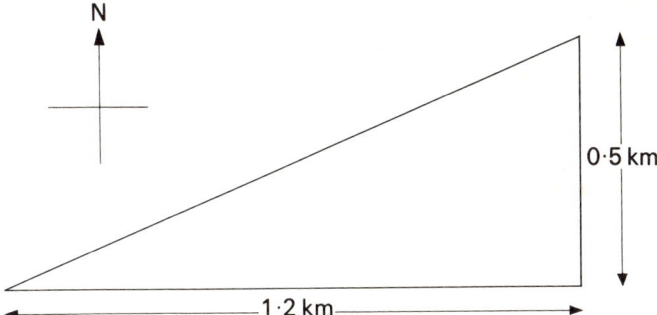

This way of representing vector quantities is so useful that it is the normal way to show them. You have used a (small) displacement to represent a (large) displacement, but later in the course you will use displacements to represent other vector quantities.

Part b

▶Considering the displacement above, find the actual distance involved. You can do this in two different ways. What are they? What is the mathematical pattern which you can use here? If you know the distance, what else must you know in order to specify the displacement completely?◀

Investigation 13.2 Displacements in three dimensions

Part a

▶So far you have been thinking of displacements in one plane, which can be represented by vectors with two components. How many components would be needed to represent a journey within a block of flats?◀

▶What is the maximum number of components needed in a vector to represent any displacement in space? Use your answer to explain the statement 'We live in a 3-D world'.◀

Figure 13.3
To reach the penthouse flat in a certain block of flats, starting at the entrance, involves moving 40 m forwards, 30 m to the right, and 120 m upwards

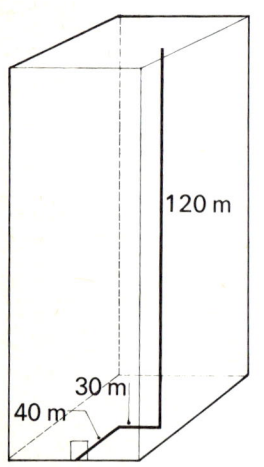

Part b

▶How could you find the actual distance from the entrance of the block of flats (see figure 13.3) to the penthouse flat? Once more there are two different ways. It is not particularly useful to know the straight line distance from the entrance to the flat! Find some examples where this sort of calculation is useful and important. ◀

▷ **Investigation 13.3 Planned movements**

Part a

The photograph and plan in figure 13.4 show a typical modern kitchen on which a considerable amount of money has clearly been spent. Has it been spent wisely, you may wonder. It may look good, but is it convenient to use? One of the things a well-planned kitchen will do is to reduce to a minimum the amount of walking about which the housewife has to do.

▶Choose a job done in the kitchen which involves moving between several points. Make a list of the movements needed to complete the job. (What is the best way of doing this?) Turn these movements into displacements (lines) drawn on a tracing of the kitchen plan, and consider whether the amount of movement is excessive. Plan a rearrangement of the kitchen, and see if you can reduce the total amount of movement required. ◀ Explain why the arrangement which minimises the movement for the job you have chosen may not in fact be the best arrangement.

Figure 13.4

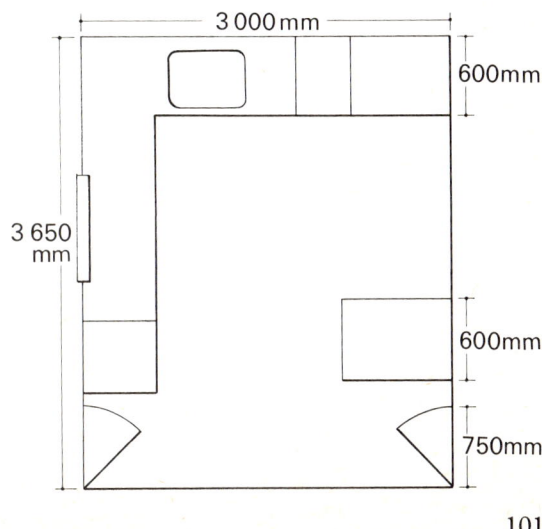

Part b

Are there aspects of kitchen planning for which a scientific approach would not be sensible? If so, what are they? You could discuss the differences between the 'ideal kitchens' of various members of your class.

Part c

To what extent do the ideas you have worked out for kitchens apply in other situations, for example, in a school or a factory? Discuss whether the plan of your laboratory, or your whole school, could be improved. Without replanning the school, how could the amount of movement between lessons be reduced? Is reducing the amount of movement necessarily the best idea?

Part d

To avoid tiredness, promote efficiency and save time, factories and workshops have developed carefully planned assembly lines. You can imagine the chaos which would result if workers were left to fetch and carry their own components in a haphazard fashion! Modern assembly line production is the result of applying

Figure 13.5

An assembly line in a motor-car factory. The cars move slowly along the line. At each position a part is added to the vehicle. Parts are brought to the correct position along the sides of the line and stored for easy acess

scientific methods (time and motion study) to the patterns of work in a factory. Independent observers make a careful assessment of such things as movements, time taken to do a job, and the tiredness of people involved. These observations may result in suggested improvements which are then tried out. But although much factory work is organised to be highly efficient and labour saving the 'human' side of the situation is equally important. What problems could be expected in factories which have highly planned work patterns, so that jobs tend to be very simple and repetitive? What could be done to overcome these problems?

It has often been suggested that people who work on an assembly line, doing tasks which are repetitive and which do not require much skill or judgment, have been reduced almost to the level of machines. However, there is no shortage of people wishing to do these (often well-paid) jobs. Discuss the reasons for this, and whether the suggestion is a reasonable one. Would you like to work on an assembly line? Assembly lines can be designed so that most of the jobs normally performed by men are done automatically by machines. Only a very few people are needed to supervise such assembly lines, and there would be no need for people to do tedious, repetitive jobs. Discuss the advantages and disadvantages of introducing this sort of automation.

Investigation 13.4 Measuring speed

Part a

 ▶ Sometimes we are interested in distance or in displacement. More often we want to know something about time as well. For example, suppose the train journey from London to Birmingham (about 150 km) takes 100 minutes (i.e. 6 000 s). What can be calculated from these figures? Which is involved, distance or displacement? ◀ What is the pattern (relation) you have to use to do the calculation?
▶ The following table gives possible values of the distance of the locomotive from its starting point at the stated times. These data are represented on the graph (see figure 13.6):

time/s	0	1 000	2 000	3 000	4 000	5 000	6 000
distance/km	0	15	50	85	105	120	150

What is the average speed for the second half (in time) of the journey? What is the average speed for the last fifth (in distance)?

Figure 13.6

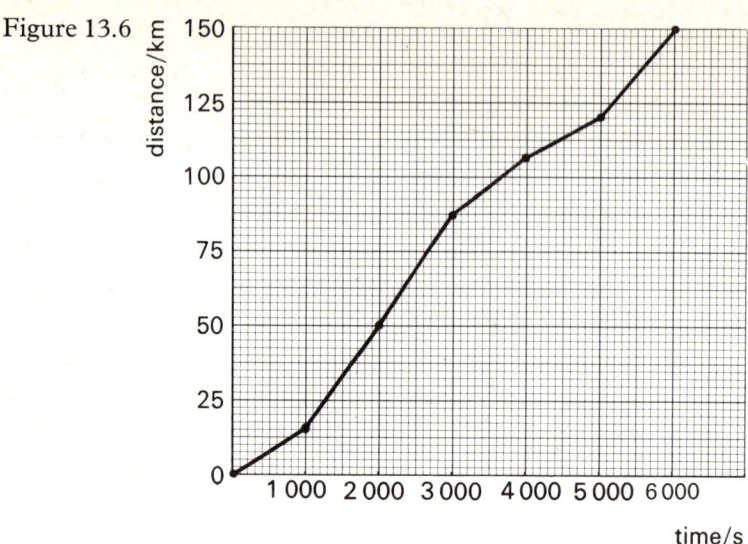

Can you tell when or whether the train stopped on the way? What can you say about the speed of the train over a particular part of the track (say the kilometre just before Watford station)? What extra measurements would be needed to find the speed over this section? What precisely is it that can be calculated from these extra measurements? ◄

Figure 13.7

Part b

▶ The table below gives some (imaginary) data for the position of the front of a train over a shorter distance, which could be part of the same journey:

time/s	1 000	1 020	1 040	1 060	1 080	1 100	1 120
distance/m	15 000	15 200	15 500	15 900	16 350	16 800	17 300

What is the average speed for the first 500 m? For the last 40 s? For the whole 120 s? Can you tell when or whether the train stopped? To answer that question what piece of everyday knowledge did you use? Can you tell exactly where the train was at time 1 030 s? Can you tell exactly when it was at position 16 200 m?

In the graph shown in figure 13.8 a smooth curve has been drawn through the points. Why is this a sensible thing to do? Why would it not be a sensible thing to do on the graph in figure 13.6? Can you be sure that the smooth curve on figure 13.8 represents the position of the train at different times accurately? Explain your answer. ◀

Figure 13.8

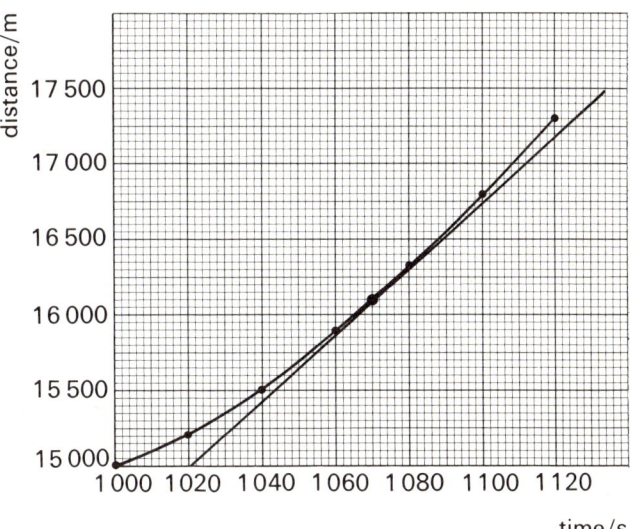

Part c

▶ Suppose you wanted to know how fast the train was travelling at time 1 070 s, or at 15 400 m. Could you find this exactly from the information given? Could you estimate it?

a Calculate from figure 13.8 the average speed between 1 065 s and 1 075 s.

b Calculate from the tangent drawn at 1 070 s the instantaneous speed at this instant. Give two different reasons why this can be only approximate. ◀

Part d

It may seem at first sight that there is an easy way round the difficulties in measuring speed: use a speedometer! Why does this suggestion not really solve the basic problem? If you have difficulty answering that question, it will help you to think out how to check the accuracy of a speedometer. You could possibly carry out the experiment. It is not difficult on a motorway. A speedometer is not much use if it is incorrect!

Figure 13.9

Part e

▷Plot a graph of a car journey to show how speed varies with time, and describe the variation in words. The scale shown in figure 13.10 will help you convert from miles per hour to $m\,s^{-1}$.

Figure 13.10

speed/mile h⁻¹

0	10	20	30	40	50	60	70
	5	10	15	20	25	30	

speed/m s⁻¹

Figure 13.11

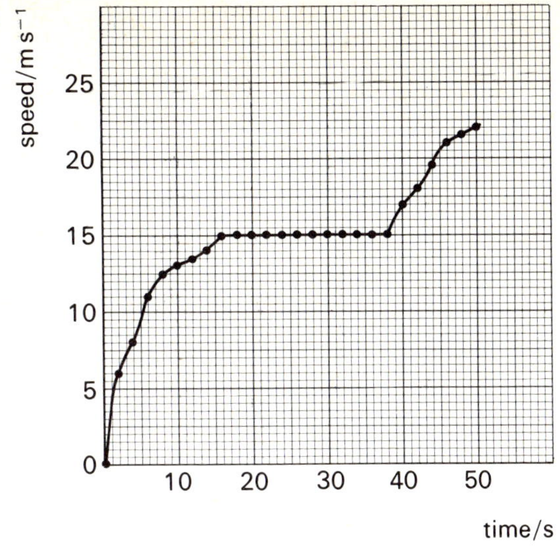

Part f

▷ ▶ The graph shown in figure 13.11 gives the results of one such experiment. Notice that this graph has speed plotted on the vertical axis (the previous ones had distance).

time/s	0	2	4	6	8	10	12	14	16	18	20	22	24
speed/m s^{-1}	0	6.0	8.0	11.0	12.5	13.0	13.5	14.0	15.0	15.0	15.0	15.0	15.0

time/s	26	28	30	32	34	36	38	40	42	44	46	48	50
speed/m s^{-1}	15.0	15.0	15.0	15.0	15.0	15.0	15.0	17.0	18.0	19.5	21.0	21.5	22.0

What is the distance travelled between 20 s and 30 s? What pattern did you use? Look at the graph in figure 13.11 and find what would represent this distance. Extend this idea to other parts of the graph. Can distance be represented in this way for every part of the graph? ◀

Part g

▷ ▶ Figure 13.12 shows the construction of a car speedometer. The cable from the transmission of the car (connected to the wheels) causes the magnet to rotate as shown at a speed proportional to the speed of the car. Use the patterns of electromagnetism to explain how this gives an indication on the dial. The following questions will help you:

Figure 13.12

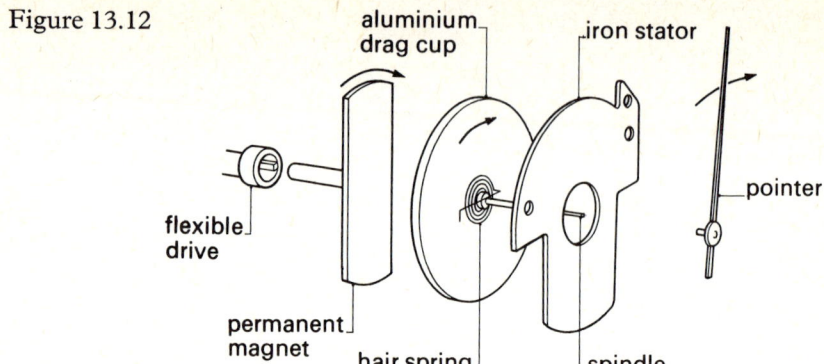

a What is the effect of the moving magnetic field of the magnet on the aluminium cup?
b What interaction will this lead to?
c What motion of the cup will result?
d What restrains the motion of the cup? ◀

Investigation 13.5 Measuring time

If we calculate speed from measurements of distance and time, the latter is usually more tricky. Measuring time has presented problems for a long while. You may have heard that Galileo found that the time of swing of a chandelier did not depend on the size of the swing, but he had to use his own pulse as a clock! (He was in church at the time, but the sermon was obviously not a compelling one.)

Make a list of the instruments available in your laboratory for measuring time, indicating for each the shortest and, where appropriate, the longest interval which it can measure. Are any of these suitable for special situations?

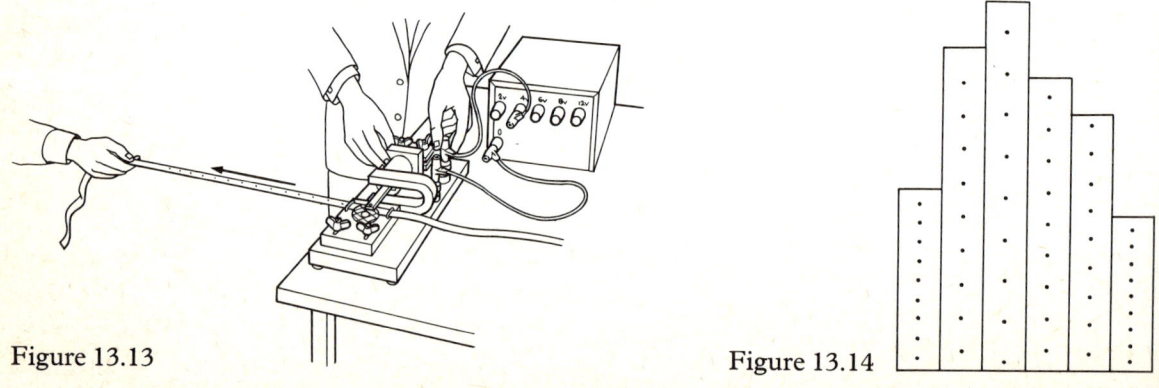

Figure 13.13

Figure 13.14

Figure 13.15
Figure 13.16

Three techniques which are probably new to you are also available: the 'ticker-timer', the electric stopclock and stroboscopic photography.

Part a   Ticker-timer

This is a device (see figure 13.13) which produces dots on a paper tape at a fixed frequency (usually 50 Hz). To measure a short interval of time all you need to do is count the spaces between the dots. The tape also enables you to measure distance, so speed can easily be calculated.

▶Use the ticker-timer to measure your own speed and then the speed of a dynamics trolley moving in various ways. The tape can be cut up so that each strip contains five dot intervals to produce what is in effect a graph of average speed against time (see figure 13.14). Work out what the scales on the two axes of your graph should be.◀

▶Once started, how does the motion of a trolley moving along the bench (or a runway) alter? Use the ticker-timer to find the answer. What is the cause of this change? Devise a way of compensating for it. How will you know when your compensation is sufficient?◀

Part b   Electric stopclock

There are several versions of this (see figures 13.15–17): small and large dial clocks controlled by mains frequency, and an electronic oscillator (usually 1 000 Hz) linked to a counter. The dial clocks can be read to 0.01 second. What is the limit of accuracy of the oscillator/counter? Your teacher will demonstrate the use of one of these. You might like to suggest suitable moving objects whose

Figure 13.17

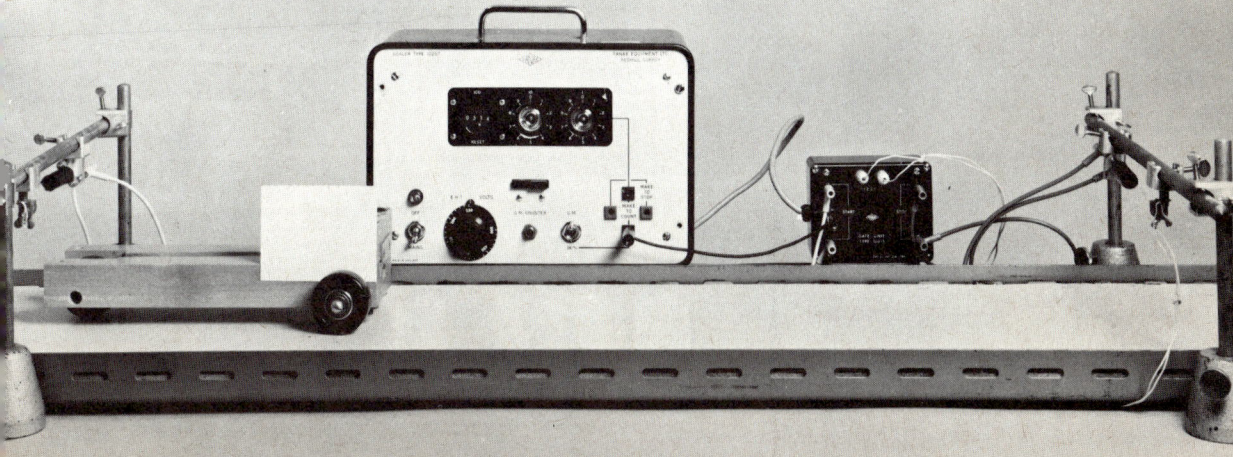

average speed could be measured. An interesting project would be to devise a way to measure people's reaction-time using the electric stopclock.

Part c   Stroboscopic photography

The photograph (see figure 13.18) shows a picture of a golfer hitting a ball. The shutter was left open and the strobe lamp was flashing at 48 Hz. Calculate the speed of the head of the club just before it hit the ball. For what sort of situation is this technique specially appropriate?

An alternative to using a strobe lamp is to illuminate the object brightly and spin a slotted disc at a known frequency of rotation in front of the camera. Your teacher may demonstrate this technique, possibly using a linear air track or 'frictionless' pucks.

Figure 13.18

Part d   Measuring the speed of light

The diagram (see figure 13.19) shows one way to measure the speed of light. The strobe disc permits short bursts of light to pass, which can reach the detector either directly or by way of the mirrors A, B and C. (The length of the second light path has been reduced in the diagram.) The problem is to measure the difference in time taken for the two paths. Each burst of light received by the detector produces a 'blip' on the screen, and the extra time taken by the light reflected from the mirrors means it causes a 'blip' a small fraction of a second later than the direct light. If the spot moves across the screen very rapidly the two 'blips' can be separated as two peaks on the trace.

▶Calculate the speed of light from the following data:

Speed of 'spot' across oscilloscope screen $10^5\,\mathrm{m\,s^{-1}}$

Distance between the two peaks on screen   20 mm

Extra distance travelled by light via mirrors   59 m

Suggest a way to measure the speed of sound using an oscilloscope. ◀

Figure 13.19

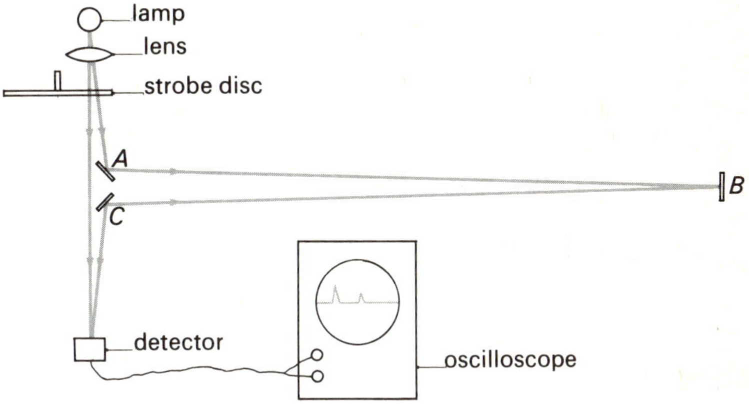

▷Part e   Improving techniques of measuring time

Write an essay about the development of techniques of time-measurement from the earliest days to the present. You should refer to whatever encyclopaedias and other books are available to you, and you might consider a visit to a museum. Find out how a second is defined now. (The definition changed a few years ago.)

Investigation 13.6 Combining speeds

Part a

Consider this problem:

▶ 'A lunar module is travelling at $600\,\mathrm{m\,s}^{-1}$ relative to the moon. The moon is moving in its orbit around the Earth at $1\,000\,\mathrm{m\,s}^{-1}$. What is the motion of the lunar module relative to the Earth?' This problem cannot be solved as it stands. Additional information is required. What information?

Assuming that the motions do not change significantly during one second, we can change the form of the question without changing its real meaning: 'What is the combination of a displacement of $600\,\mathrm{m}$ and a displacement of $1\,000\,\mathrm{m}$?' What is incomplete in that question? What two ways are there of specifying a displacement completely?

The additional information needed to solve the problem is given in the diagram shown in figure 13.20. Now find the answer. ◀

Figure 13.20

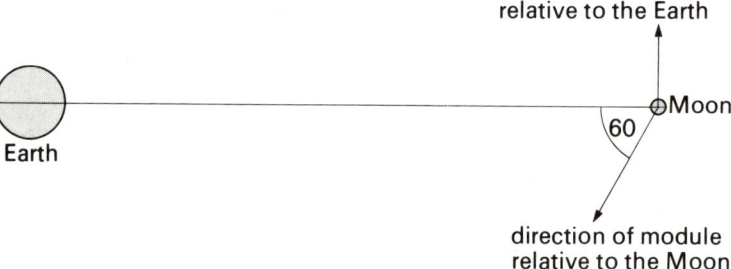

This example shows that to combine two speeds is more than a matter of simple addition. What sort of quantity were you combining? When we are interested in how rapidly something travels (for example how fast you can run) without reference to direction, we use the word speed. On the other hand, when we are concerned with the vector nature of motion (involving direction, or components) then we use the word velocity. If you understand this difference in the way the two words are used, you will probably be able to find occasions when both are used incorrectly. What about the title of this investigation?

Part b

You have already stated and used the pattern relating speed and distance. Remembering that displacement is the vector quantity which corresponds to distance, suggest a similar pattern relating velocity and displacement. Are the two patterns restricted to any particular building blocks, or can they be applied to the motion of all building blocks?

Each of these patterns comes in two versions, one concerned with an average value, the other with an instantaneous value. Discussion with your teacher will help to make this clear, and show how the terms rate and gradient are used.

Part c

▶Referring to the map in the Appendix (figure A.1, p. 152), what are the components of the average velocity in the easterly, northerly and vertically upwards directions in the following cases? Horizontal components are in 100-metre units, vertical components in metres.

i Oak Bank School (836, 155, 61) to Matson's House (848, 155, 61) in 20 minutes (walking).

ii Chambers' Farm (829, 116, 46) to Kimsbury House (865, 130, 82) in 10 minutes (by car).

What is the actual average velocity in i? How would you find the velocity (including direction) in ii? Do not forget that the heights use a different unit. ◀

Part d

▶A yacht sails at $4.0\,\mathrm{m\,s^{-1}}$ in a direction N. 30° W. through the water, but there is a current of $1.5\,\mathrm{m\,s^{-1}}$ running due east. What is the resultant velocity of the yacht (i.e. its velocity relative to the land)? ◀

Part e

▶A man in a low flying aircraft travelling at $100\,\mathrm{m\,s^{-1}}$ fires a rifle which is accurately aimed at a building 200 m away at the same height (see figure 13.21). If the speed of the bullet is $500\,\mathrm{m\,s^{-1}}$, by how much does he miss his target? ◀

Figure 13.21

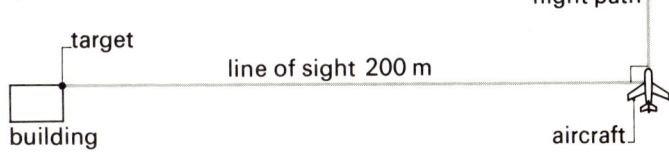

Part f

▶Think of some other examples where it is necessary to combine velocities. In each example what is the special case where the velocities can be combined 'by arithmetic' instead of 'by geometry'? ◀

▷Investigation 13.7 Scalar quantities

Most of the measurements you have made in science have *not* been measurements of vectors. They have concerned what we tend to regard as 'ordinary' quantities. The name for these quantities is scalar quantities.

Make a list of scalar quantities which you know. Do this for all building blocks in *Patterns*. For each of them ask the question: 'Do negative values have any meaning?'

What is the pattern for combining scalar quantities? Use this to explain why we think of scalar quantities as 'ordinary'.

Investigation 13.8 Speed limits

These are of two sorts, those that we impose and those nature imposes!

Part a   Natural speed limits

land/km h^{-1}		water/km h^{-1}		air/km h^{-1}	
1898	63.15	1932	201.02	1945	976
1899	105.93	1939	228.11	1948	1 080
1903	124.13	1950	258.01	1953	1 212
1909	202.02	1952	287.21	1955	1 323
1922	207.88	1955	325.60	1956	1 822
1926	275.34	1957	384.74	1959	2 456
1928	334.02	1959	418.99	1965	3 318

114

1933	438.48	1967	459.00
1935	484.62		
1938	575.34		
1947	634.40		
1964	875.69		
1965	978.82	(jet powered)	

The table above shows how the maximum speeds attainable by man has increased. Is there any evidence of a trend towards a limit? What factors are important in limiting speed in each case? There seems to be a natural limit to the speed at which matter, energy or information can travel. Can you guess what it is? All the speeds mentioned so far in this investigation are well below it, but electrons have been brought to within a small fraction of 1 per cent of this limit. Curious things happen at these speeds: you may like to read more about them in such books as *Mr Tomkins in paperback* by George Gamow.

Figure 13.22
British Rail's Advanced
Passenger Train (APT)

Part b   Speed limits on rails

Figure 13.22 shows British Rail's new Advanced Passenger Train

(APT) which will run on existing tracks and will be capable of speeds up to 150 miles per hour ($240 \, \text{km h}^{-1}$, $67 \, \text{m s}^{-1}$). This will operate first on the East Coast line between London and Edinburgh, in direct competition with aircraft. In 1972 the fastest train journey between London and Edinburgh took 5 hours 45 minutes and cost £6.60. The same journey by air took 1 hour 20 minutes and cost £11. British Rail hope to reduce the time of the rail journey to 3 hours 45 minutes on the APT. What are the advantages of each method of travel?

Part c   Speed limits on roads

Conduct a survey of speed limits on roads in your area and discuss whether they are well-placed. You might like to extend the survey to see to what extent the limits are exceeded.

Some people suggest that speed limits are not a good system, because the maximum safe speed of a vehicle depends on many factors. List these factors and discuss the arguments for and against that opinion. Some years ago the Automobile Association came out against the introduction of an experimental 70 mile-per-hour speed limit on all motorways in Britain. What are the arguments against such an experiment? (They did not succeed, and the limit is now established.)

While some people argue for and against speed limits, particularly the maximum speed limit of $70 \, \text{mile h}^{-1}$ on all roads, others have suggested that it would be better to ban very fast cars altogether. The articles which follow take opposing viewpoints. Discuss the arguments for and against fast cars. Do either of the writers ignore arguments made on the other side, or offer inadequate replies? Do they in any way overstate their cases? What, if anything, do you think should be done?

Traditionally the motor industry has strongly supported motor racing, but such sponsorship is now decreasing, and firms with no obvious connection with motoring are acting as sponsors. What reasons can you suggest for this change? Is the emphasis on speed and performance in car advertisements likely to have any undesirable side-effects? If so, what could be done about it?

Not criminal

The Guardian last week published an article called "The Criminal Classes" (i.e. motorists) which severely criticized manufacturers for continuing to build fast cars and motorists for buying them and using this speed — if they do. Since it is the sort of article which will be widely quoted by RoSPA and the Pedestrians Association, if no one else, we have to say that it doesn't seem to us to be very accurate.

First of all the author dismisses the export case for fast cars. Any speed over 70 mph is illegal in Britain and "within a few short years" he says "it is certain that it will be illegal in most other countries." Where this certainty comes from we don't know. Even in America such states as Nevada have no maximum limit and on French, German and Italian motorways speeds below 70 mph are unusual except for inherently slow vehicles.

Then he goes on to dismiss as "nonsense" the claim that fast cars can overtake safely and accelerate out of trouble if a hazard presents itself, ". . . the man who relies on power to keep him out of trouble is first a bad driver and second a driver courting disaster." Well, we must be all those things because we feel so much safer in cars with vivid acceleration every time we overtake anything at all. Not only is the time of exposure so much less but also one becomes almost independent of the vagaries of the man you are overtaking who may (and often does) accelerate himself in the apparent hope that you will have a head-on collision with someone coming the other way. Many people, with less powerful cars, we notice, have either given up overtaking or else do it in sheer frustration in the worst possible places.

Finally, what about the legal argument? "If there is a speed limit in operation . . . it is there to be obeyed." This argument was equally valid in the red flag days or so when applied to the 20 mph overall speed limit which lasted for decades after it ceased to be observed. If a law is a bad one and unrealistic it will quite rightly cease to be obeyed. We know of nothing which lends divine authority to the figure of 70 mph and indeed we have published a great deal of evidence in the past to show that overall limits of this sort have little or no effect on the accident rate.

The criminal classe

by IAN BREACH

IN JUST OVER two weeks' time it will be possible to drive without interruption from Hendon, in north London, to Carlisle. The opening of the last seven-mile section of the Midland Link at Gravelly Hill Interchange will connect the M1 and M6 motorways to give an unbroken stretch of nearly 300 miles and turn a journey that, even ten years ago, could last for eight or nine hours into one that can be done comfortably in half the time with a coffee stop thrown in.

That assumes observance of the speed limit, for there are a great many cars capable of covering that distance in three hours, a handful of doing it in two. The Motor's performance summary lists 65 cars sold in Britain that have a top speed over 100 mph or more; ten can exceed 125 mph, and two are equipped with the power to travel at more than two and half miles a minute. The list is by no means comprehensive or even consistent, including the Lamborghini Jarama (162 mph) but omitting the Jaguar EV12 (145 mph).

Now everyone knows that it is illegal in Britain to drive on the public highways at these speeds; many realise, too, that within a few short years it is certain that it will be illegal in most other countries. The argument, therefore, that exports to countries where no restrictions exist is good reason for producing 100 mph-plus

models in Britain will not hold water for very much longer. But with very few exceptions, the public and the motor industry accept what seems to me to be a bizarre and unsatisfactory state of affairs.

British Leyland points to the fact that the EV12, which can exceed the limit applicable to most American roads by 80 mph, cannot be made in anything like the numbers demanded by US customers. So, the argument seems to be, they are obviously buying it in spite of the fact that they cannot lawfully use even half of the car's potential: one presumes that the marketing men at Jaguar feel that the illicit output itself is a main attraction. If this is so, it mean that Jaguar are exploiting and furthering a disagreeable human failing.

I make no apology for labouring the point. If there is a speed limit in operation in most developed countries it is there to be obeyed. The laxness with which it happens to be enforced in countries like Britain and Germany is no excuse for continuing to manufacture quite wastefully overpowered engines. It is an excuse cheerfully embraced by many in the motor industry: "No one takes much notice of the limit, do they?" ask the public-relations men.

But most people do. A short trip along any motorway will confirm that the vast majority of drivers stay well within the maximum, not because their cars lack the mechanical ability to go faster, but because they feel happier to drive at speeds of

65 mph or so than to hug the outside lane in the 80s and 90s. They seem to accept the old RoSPA catchphrase: my arguments with that organisation have been many, but I accept it, too—Speed Kills. Accidents outside urban areas happen less often per mile than in the cities, but when they do happen, they are invariably very nasty ones.

The industry musters two other arguments in its case for building vehicles able to break the laws with ease. One is that such cars can overtake safely and accelerate out of trouble if a hazard presents itself. To which I say nonsense; speeds, like most other things in life, are relative, and the man who relies on power to keep him out of trouble is first a bad driver and second a driver courting disaster.

Their other answer is that an engine running at measurably less than full rated output is likely to perform more smoothly, efficiently, and quietly—and for longer. If this were true it would be an indictment of engine designers or, more probably, those who give them their design brief. But it isn't by any means wholly true. Skimped insulation and cost-cutting bodywork design is responsible for most of the noise excess in comparatively low-powered cars. As for engine life and efficiency, what is wrong with the Mini or the Fiat 850—both which can be run for hours at 65-70 mph without strain?

The Americans, accustomed to squandering their money and resources on engines of four, five, and six litres, have ideas of limiting speed by the use of cut-outs, alarm bells, flashing lights, and God-knows what other extra technology, when all that needs doing is to make smaller engines. The savings could be spent on making cars more reliable, more durable, more safe, and less noisy. This is not wishful thinking: it is bound to happen eventually, but like most advances in the industry, it will come years after it was possible.

Recently there have been mutterings, inside and outside Parliament, about the admissibility of promotional material which mentions top speeds of more than 70 m.p.h. To be fair, manufacturers have dropped the accent on speed in their advertisements. But many have not, and the Public Interest Research Centre and the International Federation of Pedestrians have been considering whether to raise the issue at governmental level. Official reaction, I am afraid, is likely to be diluted: little progress will be made until the industry itself removes the glamour of power and speed from motoring and stops fostering connections—physical and psychological—between everyday driving and racing or rallying.

The freedom to travel en masse from London to Carlisle in four and a half hours has been bought at great social cost. To do it in less time, other than by rail (and even that begs the question of what one does with the costly minutes saved) is unreasonable and unnecessary.

Figure 13.23
Holidays on canals are becoming increasingly popular

Part d Speed limits on water

Try to find out if there are any speed limits on waterways in your area. What possible reasons are there for these?

Part e Speed limits in the air

Supersonic transports (SSTs) are now flying, and over long distances will roughly halve the flying time required by subsonic aircraft, assuming they are able to fly supersonically most of the time. Several considerations make this saving of time seem more valuable than it really is. The following will illustrate the point.

Figure 13.24
'Concordski', the Russian TU-144 supersonic airliner

▶How much time is saved on a 5 000 km flight (for example, across the Atlantic) by increasing the average speed from 500 km h^{-1} (typical of piston-engined aircraft) to 1 000 km h^{-1} (typical of subsonic jet aircraft)? How much time is saved by increasing the average speed from 1 000 km h^{-1} to 2 000 km h^{-1} (typical of SSTs)?

The total time spent on the journey may be much longer than the actual flying time. The times given below are typical of a transatlantic journey:

from home to departure airport	40 minutes
departure procedures (customs, registration, boarding, waiting, etc.)	40 minutes
arrival procedures (customs, etc.)	20 minutes
from arrival airport to destination	50 minutes
	$2\frac{1}{2}$ hours

▶What percentage of the total journey time is saved by using a SST instead of a subsonic jet aircraft?◀

The cost of an Atlantic return crossing is much more by SST than by a scheduled flight on a subsonic aircraft. Charter flights can cost less than half scheduled flights. Under what circumstances would you buy a ticket to travel by SST?

There is a considerable 'lobby' expressing strong views against SSTs, in the forefront of which is the 'Anti-Concorde Project'. On 18 May 1970 this organisation took an advertisement in *The Times*, part of which is reproduced in figure 13.25. Discuss the facts and arguments put forward. Several of the items are now out of date, but the general arguments remain. The advertisement naturally does not put the arguments in favour of Concorde. What are some of these? Are the points made in the advertisement overstated, or are they (as far as you can tell) a fair assessment of the position? Should people be allowed to campaign against projects like the Concorde which will bring employment to many people? Is it so complex that the decisions should be left to those in authority?

Figure 13.25

The objections to supersonic transport may be summarised:

1 ENVIRONMENTAL AND SOCIOLOGICAL PROBLEMS ARISING MAINLY FROM:
(i) the sonic bang; (ii) airport noise; (iii) hazards to passengers and crews; (iv) effects of pollution —especially in the upper atmosphere.

2 THE IMMENSE COST OF THE SST PROJECTS—the spending of prodigious sums of public money (other sources of capital being unable and unwilling to provide support); the diversion of immense resources (financial, material, technological, intellectual) away from more useful and profitable enterprises—and from essential human, national and international needs.

1 **(i) THE SONIC BANG.** This is a shock wave (analogous to the bow wave of a ship) which is *generated continuously throughout the entire length of supersonic flight* (not, as is still commonly believed, only at the instant of "breaking the sound barrier"). The resulting disturbance and damage are well documented in many reports, especially from the U.S.A. and France. (REFS. 5, 6, 7).

RESONANCE. The report of an investigation by the Ministry of Public Building and Works' Building Research Station (REF. 9) suggests that in the causation of damage to buildings, *resonance* may be a more significant factor than *overpressure*, with the result that sonic bangs of 2 lb./sq. FOOT may be as damaging as bomb-blast of 2 lb./sq. INCH. (This situation occurs when harmonics resulting from components of the shock wave coincide with the vibration periods of parts of buildings). The implications of this report—which has received almost no publicity—are alarming.

(ii) AIRPORT NOISE. When Concorde was commenced it was assumed that airport noise levels would continue to rise, unabated. But people living near airports are past the limits of endurance. New regulations aim to cut take-off and landing noise by half, and to control runway noise. Supersonic aircraft cannot meet the proposed standards. Concorde has therefore had to be exempted from the British proposals—but will other governments exempt it? "U.S. noise standards could conceivably bar the Concorde from access to the principal U.S. international airports, which would undoubtedly doom the Concorde programme." (REF. 2, PAGE H.16435).

(iii) HAZARDS TO PASSENGERS AND CREWS. "Passengers and crew will be vulnerable to a number of potentially serious physical, physiological and psychological stresses associated with rapid acceleration, gravitational changes, reduced barometric pressure, increased ionising radiation, temperature changes, and aircraft noise and vibration." (REF. 2, PAGE H.16435).

(iv) EFFECTS OF POLLUTION—ESPECIALLY IN UPPER ATMOSPHERE. "The widespread use of supersonic transport will introduce large quantities of water vapour into the stratosphere . . . [This] can produce two effects which may be important:

(1) Persistent contrails might form to such an extent that there would be a significant increase in cirrus clouds;

(2) There could be a significant increase in the relative humidity of the stratosphere even if there were no significant increase in the extent of cirrus cloudiness. Both effects would alter the radiation balance and thereby possibly affect the general circulation of atmospheric components."—REF. 2, PAGES H 16436-7). The possible long-term effects are unpredictable, but many meteorologists and geophysicists have pointed out that changes in the weather and climate could result. We have already polluted the environment—locally and globally—in very many ways, some of which have already resulted in seriously dangerous situations.

TURNING WORLD RESOURCES INTO WORLD POLLUTION.

We know that if we continue to add to this pollution, before long we shall have an uninhabitable world. *We are turning world resources into world pollution at an ever-increasing rate.* Supersonic transport would be another step up in this process—just as we are realizing that the process must be stepped down if the world is to remain habitable. The fuel consumption of Concorde per passenger-mile is 2½ times that of subsonic aircraft. Aviation fuel contains many poisonous additives. SST would pollute new areas—the upper atmosphere. To do without SST would be a good beginning to the act of curbing our worst, most wasteful and most pointless excesses. *Political expediency—or timidity—in this matter could have disastrous long-term results.*

STRONG PUBLIC REACTION.

A strong public reaction against all forms of pollution of the environment has commenced. Aircraft noise is recognized as a form of pollution; there is unlikely to be a spirit of acquiescence or resignation to the menace of sonic bangs. Sonic bang pollution is compounded by the effects referred to above, and again by the fact that smoke pollution at airports is now recognized as a major problem. SSTs produce far more smoke than other aircraft. This, again, will not be tolerated.

2 THE COST OF CONCORDE

(1 to 5) Progressive estimates of the cost of research and development for Concorde.

(1) Estimate for the Supersonic Transport Aircraft Committee (1959).

(2) Estimate at the time of the Anglo-French Concorde Agreement (1962).

(3 to 5) Subsequent revised estimates. The 1969 estimate *excludes* the cost of establishing the production line and a reserve for "contingencies"—both included in some previous estimates. (Production line financing now estimated at £200m.). **The research and development costs are now admitted to be irrecoverable.**

(6) The cost limit proposed by the Minister of Technology in May 1969.

(7) The amount already spent.

(8 & 9) The result of a "successful" outcome of the Concorde project (with 200 machines sold) showing

(8) **Selling price (incl. spares):** **£2,600m.**
    (a) Production costs: £2,200m.
    (b) Manufacturers' profits: £400m.

(9) **Total costs:** **£3,200m.**
    (i) Production costs: £2,200m.
    (ii) Pre-production costs (irrecoverable — therefore a Loss to British and French governments and people): £1,000m.

The figures in (8) and (9) are probably biassed in favour of the Concorde. Higher costs for development or production, or lower profits or sales figures, would of course increase the loss.

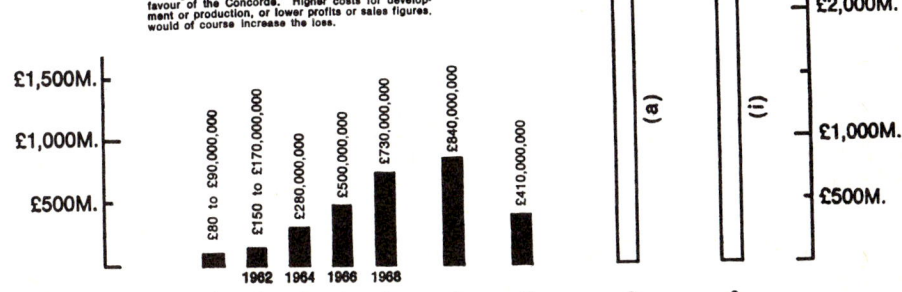

121

Continued from page 4

CANCEL THE

FALLACIES

We submit that the facts stated on the opposite page support the conclusi
that advocacy for supersonic transport has, from the beginning, be
characterized by grossly inadequate estimates of cost, by extravagant a
insubstantiable claims about its benefits, and by refusal to face the fa
about its antisocial effects.   As a result the subject is wreathed in fallaci
Some of these are briefly noted here.

TIME-SAVING FALLACIES

1. Saving three hours on a transatlantic flight—the reduction of journey time between city centres from about 10 hours to about 7 hours—is claimed as an immense advance. But far fewer than 1% of the people of even the wealthiest nations are regular travellers on intercontinental flights—and few of these would travel by Concorde.

Incomparably greater savings of time and increases of efficiency, benefiting immensely greater numbers of people, could be obtained by spending a small fraction of the cost of SST projects on (for example) improving the increasingly inadequate and chaotic conditions of public transport on the ground.

2. Cost-benefit analysis reveals that while the 100 supersonic passengers were saving 2 or 3 hours each (say 300 man-hours) on the flight, the time *wasted* by disturbance of people by sonic bang *would exceed this by a factor of hundreds or thousands*

3. "*Day trips to New York*" fallacy. Such a trip would involve 7 hours (minimum) flying—at least 13 hours travelling.

Day Trips to Europe from the U.S.A.

An American businessman making an early start (9.0 a.m. take-off from New York) would arrive in London at around 19.00 hours (London time). Presumably he would have travelled in order to work and not merely to dine; and that his hosts would be willing to prolong their working day well into the night.

To return to New York airport by midnight (to preserve the concept of a "day trip") it would be necessary to take-off by 1.30 a.m. (London time)—waking half of west London in the process

Privileged Minority

It is unlikely that "top executives" would impose this ordeal upon themselves. "Transatlantic day trips" would become another burden upon "middle executives". Our information is that those who are aware of this possibility regard it with dread.

Faster Forms of Communication

A direct-dialling transatlantic telephone service has commenced. This service may spread until it is world-wide. With loud speaking telephones and television link-up added, there will be little incentive for supersonic day trips to New York.

PROFITABILITY FALLACY

Highly favourable claims about potential profits on sales of Concordes have been made. For example, B.A.C. claims (in an "aide memoire" issued in March, 1969):

"*A sale of 250 Concordes would bring into the UK. and France some £2,000 million each in foreign currency over the operating life of the aircraft. (This figure includes, in addition to the proceeds of export sales, the net overseas earnings of home-based Concordes.*"

This figure does not, however, include the adverse effects upon the U.K. and French balance of payments of the operations of 230 *foreign-owned* Concordes; nor is any reference made to the fact that each Concorde sold to a foreign air-

line for £13 millions (including spa would have cost (including developmen least £15 million of taxpayers' money produce—£2 million of this having to paid out in dollars for equipment chased in the U.S.A. (REF. 8, PAGE

DEMAND FALLACY

In the early 1960s international air tr was increasing rapidly. It was assu that this trend would continue ind nitely. But the increase has fallen o already half the seats on scheduled fli are empty. Price-cutting has started the transatlantic routes—and will incre as more passengers are demanded by "jumbos". These have been conceiv built and put into operation since Concorde was commenced. They ar formidable new form of competitio vastly more spacious and comforta than the Concorde; quicker than o subsonic aircraft (and apparently not m noisy at airports); they have far gre range than Concorde (or other S.S. and of course are not subject to so bang restrictions.

Supersonic travel is inherently more pensive than subsonic. Unless there a dramatic and unexpected increase in travel at first-class prices on transoce routes, airlines contemplating buying C cordes would face these options: (i) raise fares on their "jumbos" to su dise the Concordes—and reduce the n ber of jumbo passengers; (ii) to buy C cordes for "prestige" and fly them a vast loss; (iii) to force down the sel price of Concorde to a "giveaway" le —thereby reducing their operating los

CONCORDE

the expense of the British and French
ayers.

WE DON'T BUILD THE
NCORDE WILL THE
ERICANS "SCOOP THE
.T. MARKET"?

re are very strong reasons for expecting
t if the Concorde is cancelled, the U.S.
.T. will be cancelled. The "chal-
ze of the Concorde" is the main line
efence for the U.S. project. The view
widely held in American aviation and
ernment that no substantial S.S.T.
ket exists.

O LATE TO STOP
E CONCORDE?

y suggestion that it is too late to stop
Concorde "because it has flown"—
for any other reason—is fallacious.
s than half of the £1,000 *millions*
uired for research and development
been spent.
ny problems remain. The Concorde is
y far from being a *fait accompli*—and
American SST even further.
re basic still is the fact that if these
chines were ever introduced into
ration, their sonic bangs would en-
der immediate, massive and cumula-
e demands that they should be stopped.
the U.K. the campaign against SSTs
grown to its present strength before
ingle SST sonic bang has been heard.
e outrage of the bangs will provide
focus for "environmental" protests
m the most orthodox to the most
itant.

UPERSONIC TRANSPORT—
IT PROGRESS?

e welcome technological innovations
t improve the quality of people's lives.
some people, all technological innova-
n is necessarily synonymous with "pro-
ss"; in our view this assumption is
lacious.

TECHNOLOGICAL
ALL-OUT"

is claimed that the Concorde has
ought great benefits in "technological
l-out". These claims are vague, in-
dequately documented, and probably

highly exaggerated, but in so far as such
"fall-out" can result from the Concorde
project (by the development of new
materials, new techniques, &c.), this has
already been achieved and so will be
unaffected by early cancellation. All these
benefits could have been obtained by
direct research at a fraction of the cost
of the SST projects.

THE "PRESTIGE" FALLACY

The advocates of supersonic transport
claim that the building of these machines
will bring prestige. In what way the
promotion of these vastly antisocial and
apparently inevitably unprofitable projects,
producing machines of minimal usefulness for which—even after immense sales
promotion efforts—there is minimal
demand, can possibly be productive of
prestige, has never been explained.

DO THE AIRLINES WANT
CONCORDE?

In spite of immense efforts by a large
special sales staff (established early in
1968) the number of "options" (reserved
delivery positions) on Concorde has
remained at 74 since 1967. Of these, 24
were taken by airlines operating mainly
or entirely over the continental U.S.A.;
these are now hardly likely to become
orders, since the U.S. Government now
proposes to prohibit commercial supersonic
overflying.
The President of Pan Am has "*expressed
serious doubts*" about Concorde (REFS.
10, 11)—doubts centred upon (i) *profit-
ability*—limited range, small capacity,
high fares; (ii) *technical points* about the
accessibility of components for maintenance; (iii) *operational problems* including
sonic bang, airport noise and smoke
emission.
"If Pan Am lets its options slide, others
might be tempted to follow suit since
most airlines are having troubles digesting
the capacity they already have. . . .
Many airlines have expressed concern that,
as the Concorde's weight has increased, its
ability to cross the North Atlantic non-
stop with anything more than a 'face-
saving' number of passengers was in
doubt." (REF. 10.)
The President of Pan Am suggested that
a very much enlarged version of the
Concorde should be produced. To environ-
mentalists this is unthinkable—and the
British and French taxpayers may well
agree.

THE FRANKENSTEIN
SYNDROME

The Concorde of 1970 is very different
from the concept that, in order to gain
government support, was advocated so
vigorously by the aviation interests in the
early 1960s. Government support was
obtained for proposals which were remarkably dissimilar from the reality. The
prodigious rises in the cost of development are shown in the figure (page 4). The
machine itself has become larger and
heavier: it will therefore generate a sonic
bang more severe than was originally sup-
posed. A strong public reaction against
aircraft noise and other forms of pollution
is now rapidly building up

Competition

The increase of passenger traffic has fallen
below predictions. The rapid introduction
of "jumbo" jets has brought a serious
new element of competition.

Prospects

The prospects for the Concorde are
extremely poor—and if it did become a
commercial "success" this would be at
the cost of enormous antisocial consequences.
The Concorde is a classic example of the
Frankenstein syndrome; a monstrosity has
been created which is beyond both the in-
tentions and the control of its creators,
and which is revealed as an antisocial
menace.

WHY ARE THE SSTs BEING
BUILT?

If the Concorde and other SSTs are so
wrong why are they being built?

It is often said that without the Concorde
the "advanced" aviation industry could
not survive. If its survival truly depends
on spending public money to build
machines which the public would be better
off without, what purpose is being served?
We are forced to conclude that the con-
tinuation of such projects—on both sides
of the Atlantic—is less for the purpose of
producing usable, saleable aircraft, than
to provide support for sections of the
aircraft industry.

123

14 Classifying building blocks

So much of this course is concerned with building blocks that at some stage you must have asked the question 'why?'. The answer is simple – it is merely convenient to group things into a number of different sets called building blocks. Relations between these building blocks are shown in the diagram. Discuss the relations.

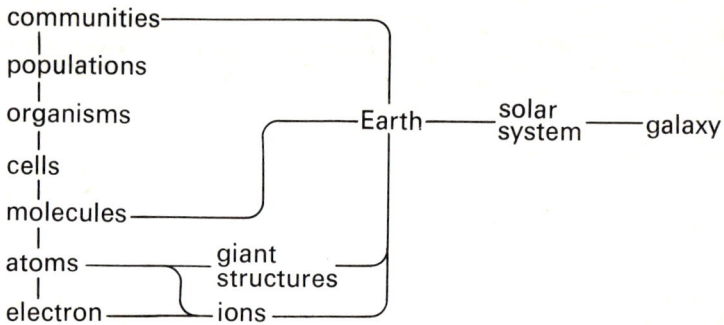

Sometimes, again only because of convenience, it is useful to consider other sets of building blocks such as rocks which are not shown above.

How many of each of the different building blocks are thought to exist? It is known that there are many millions of stars, which make up the galaxies, although there are just a few planets in our solar system. (How many planets are there round the Sun?) There are $1\frac{1}{2}$ million known types of organism; and one organism can contain hundreds of different kinds of cell.

There are millions of molecule building blocks. You can see how this is possible by looking at some of the arrangements of the carbon and hydrogen atom building blocks to produce the following six molecules:

CH_4 methane
C_2H_6 ethane
C_3H_8 propane
C_4H_{10} butane
C_5H_{12} pentane
C_6H_{14} hexane

(Incidentally, can you see a pattern in the above list?) There are just over 100 known elements and each one has its own special properties.

To enable us to deal with such an enormous variety it would obviously be useful to search for patterns which would enable the building blocks to be classified in some way.

Investigation 14.1 Classifying organisms

The patterns of classification which can emerge from studies of building blocks are man-made devices – we choose how we will group into sets and subsets. The same organism, or atom, can be classified in different ways for different purposes, or by different people. Some ways are more useful than others. In this investigation similarity of structure is used as the basis for classifying. What other bases for classifying organisms could you use? In other investigations you will use, for example, the properties of the building blocks concerned.

You will need

named specimens of living or preserved animals without backbones (and, if necessary, pictures)
hand lens

You will find several stations around the laboratory. At each station there is an animal or plant labelled with its scientific name. You will have noticed that this is made up from two words. You can find out more about this by reading the *Patterns* topic book *The diversity of life*.

Part a

Already in the organisms chosen for this investigation it is implied that organisms have been classified into three subsets. The other two would be animals with backbones (or vertebrates) and plants.

Complete a table for each of the organisms supplied similar to the one shown in figure 14.1 on page 126 by ticking the appropriate square. Using the completed table decide whether or not the organisms investigated can be classified into a small number of sets based on patterns of structural similarities and differences.

Use the topic book *The diversity of life* to name the sets or groups. Would the classification be the same if you had chosen 'habitat' as the basis on which to group the organisms? To whom might this latter classification be useful?

Figure 14.1 Animals without backbones (invertebrates)

Name of specimen												
Outside (or[1] exo-) skeleton present												
Exoskeleton absent												
Radial body (a) symmetry												
Bilateral body (b) symmetry												
Jointed walking legs present												
Jointed walking legs absent												
Body segmented (c)												
Body not segmented												
Tentacles present												
Tentacles absent												
Antennae (feelers) present												
Antennae absent												
Major group to which specimen belongs												

[1]The exoskeleton is a hard or semi-hard outer covering to the animal.

Figure 14.2
a Radial symmetry: the animal can be divided into two equal halves through any diameter

b Bilateral symmetry: the animal can be divided into two equal halves down one longitudinal axis only

c Body segmentation

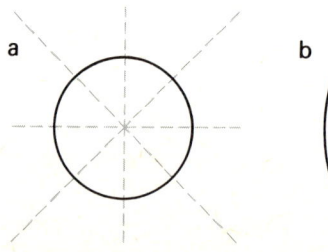
a

b

c

Part b

▶ Examine the second series of organisms provided. Do they fit into the pattern you have just devised and, if so, how? Devise a grouping system for these organisms. ◀ Discuss how this investigation could be continued and how it would end.

Investigation 14.2 Grouping people

People are grouped on the basis of similarities and differences in a number of different ways. The Registrar-General does this on the basis of jobs done by people. The following table shows a division into five social classes.

1931

social class	occupation	percentage
I	higher professional and managerial	2
II	intermediate non-manual	13
III	skilled manual and routine non-manual	49
IV	semi-skilled	18
V	unskilled	18
		100

Discuss the limitations of this classification. A different breakdown is shown below in the 1961 table:

1961

socio economic group	occupation	percentage
1	employers and managers, etc. – large establishments	3.6
2	employers and managers, etc. – small establishments	5.9
3	professional workers – self-employed	0.8
4	professional workers – employees	2.8
5	intermediate non-manual workers	3.8
6	junior non-manual	12.5

7	personal service	0.9
8	foremen and supervisors – manual	3.3
9	skilled manual workers	30.4
10	semiskilled manual workers	14.7
11	unskilled manual workers	8.6
12	own-account workers (not professional)	3.6
13	farmers – employers and managers	1.0
14	farmers – own account	1.0
15	agricultural workers	2.3
16	members armed forces	1.9
	unclassified	2.9
		100.0

However, this grouping still has its weaknesses, which you could discuss. In particular, how homogeneous is each of the groups? Are sixteen groups more convenient than five? There is an

Figure 14.3
The distribution of personal incomes in the U.K. 1966. (Number of persons in thousands)

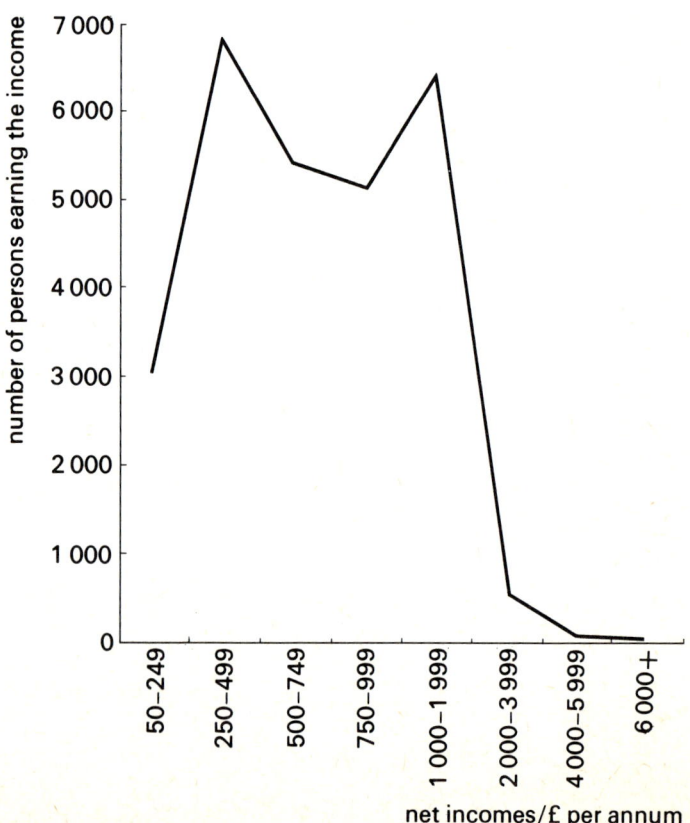

obvious progression in the 1931 grouping; is there here? A further classification is based on income (see figure 14.3). Is this useful, or helpful? Suggest how the horizontal axis could be modified to make the data less misleading.

The management of a large American chemicals company is classified according to brief cases and office desks.

Brief cases – Top dogs: none – they ask the questions.

VIPs: use backs of envelopes.

Brass: someone goes along to carry theirs.

No. 2s: carry their own – empty.

Eager-beavers: daily carry their own – filled with work.

Hoi-polloi: too poor to own one.

Office desks – Top dogs: custom made (to order).

VIPs: executive style (to order).

Brass: type A 'director'.

No. 2s: type B 'manager'.

Eager-beavers: cast-offs from no. 2s.

Hoi-polloi: yellow oak.

Similar status symbols occur in this country (for example, in the Civil Service).

Is it right to classify people in these ways? Is it necessary? Are there other ways of classifying people which are commonly used? Discuss some of the problems that are raised by such classifications.

Figure 14.4
Two other ways which have been used to group people which have produced disastrous effects

Investigation 14.3 Devising a way of identifying building blocks

You will need

set of organisms
hand lens

▶Devise a way of identifying all the individual members of your class using easily observable patterns with which you are familiar. ◀
▶Devise a way of identifying each one of the set of organisms which you have been given. ◀

▷Investigation 14.4 Devising a key for identifying certain cations

You will need

six test-tubes, 100 × 16 mm
Bunsen burner
solutions of copper nitrate, zinc nitrate, calcium nitrate, aluminium nitrate and ammonium nitrate
ammonium hydroxide solution
sodium hydroxide solution

Investigate the action (a) of sodium hydroxide solution and (b) of ammonium hydroxide solution on each of the nitrate solutions in turn. If a precipitate is obtained, add excess hydroxide to discover if the precipitate dissolves. ▶On the basis of your observations draw up a key for the identification of each of the five cations. You could test your key by asking a friend to give you a chloride formed by one of the five cations and then attempting to identify it. ◀

Investigation 14.5 Identifying organisms

You will need

any unnamed organisms from your mini-pond community
the booklet *Key to small organisms in soil, litter and water troughs*

▶Identify as many organisms as possible in the time available. ◀

Investigation 14.6 Rock identification

You will need

one conglomerate specimen ⎫
one obsidian specimen
one shale specimen
one schist specimen   These materials may be shared by a
one gabbro specimen   group
one knife-blade ⎭

You will need to refer to the *Patterns* topic book *Rocks and minerals*, where there is a key to the identification of rocks.

Make a table in your note-book as follows:

name of specimen	distinctive features	major group
obsidian, Lipari Isles	components are too small to be seen as individual particles. Rock consists of glassy material.	igneous

Using the information from the labels on the specimens and the key, fill in the details of your observations and identifications.

With the materials at your disposal consider each of the major rock groups and comment briefly on:

a the difference between the rocks within each group

b the similarities between the rocks within each group.

Figure 14.5 shows four of the various ways rocks are used in building construction. Do you like the ways they have been used?

ure 14.5

lint: a material used in chalk areas e.g. the Downs   b Marble: often used as a facing material. Why?

c Sandstone: a popular material. Why?

d Limestone: still often used to advantage in limestone areas

▷**Investigation 14.7 Life in the past**

You will need

a selection of fossil specimens (real or casts)

A number of different specimens of fossils are displayed round the laboratory for you to examine. Each specimen is labelled with its scientific name. Refer to the key of the major fossil groups in *The diversity of life* in order to complete a table like that shown below:

name of specimen (as on label)	distinctive features	which parts of the original specimen are preserved?	major group (phylum/ class, etc.)

How are the groups in which you placed the specimens related to the groups used in Investigation 1.2 and 1.3? Are there some groups you saw before, but which are not represented here?

Think of an explanation for the fact that some organisms are preserved as fossils, and others are not. Devise your own definition of a fossil.

Investigation 14.8 Classifying the atom building blocks

You will need

book of data
circuit board
one U2 cell
bulb and holder
connectors

i To observe samples of the following

arsenic
beryllium
bromine
chlorine
gallium
germanium
iodine
phosphorus (red)
potassium
sodium
strontium

ii To observe the following and to experiment with a few samples:

aluminium	silicon
antimony	sulphur
boron	tellurium
calcium	tin
carbon	neon
indium	
lithium	
magnesium	
nitrogen	
oxygen	
selenium	

	A		B	C	D	E	F
element	colour	M.P./°C	B.P./°C	physical state at room temperature	metallic lustre	conducts electricity	relative atomic mass
aluminium		660	2 400				
antimony		630	1 400				
argon		− 189	− 186				
arsenic		–	615				
beryllium		1 280	2 500				
boron		2 030	3 700				
bromine		− 7.3	58.2				
calcium		850	1 440				
carbon		3 500	3 900				
chlorine		− 101	− 34.1				
fluorine		− 220	− 188				
gallium		29.8	2 000				
germanium		958	2 800				
indium		156	2 000				
iodine		114	183				
krypton		− 157	− 153				
lithium		180	1 340				
magnesium		650	1 110				
neon		− 249	− 246				
nitrogen		− 210	− 196				
oxygen		− 219	− 183				
phosphorus		44.2	280				
potassium		63.2	760				
rubidium		38.5	700				
selenium		217	688				
silicon		1 410	2 500				
sodium		97.8	883				
strontium		770	1 380				
sulphur		119	445				
tellurium		450	1 000				
tin		232	2 600				
xenon		112	− 108				

Thirty-two of the elements have been chosen for these experiments. You will need reference books for some of them.

Part a

Complete column A of the chart. Do you think that classification by colour is useful?

Part b

Look at the melting point (M.P) and boiling point (B.P.) data in column B. Use this information to decide which elements are probably molecules at room temperature and which are probably giant structures at room temperature. Do you think that the classification 'molecule' or 'giant structure' is useful? Is it difficult to decide into which group to place certain elements?

Part c

Complete column C of the chart. Is the classification 'solid', 'liquid' and 'gas' useful? Is it difficult to decide into which group to place certain elements?

Part d

Complete column D of the chart. Is it useful to classify elements in this way? Do you have difficulty in assigning some elements?

Part e

Classify the elements as conductors or non-conductors of electricity (Column E). Are all metals conductors? Are all non-metals non-conductors? Is there a pattern? Are there exceptions to the pattern?

You need only try this experiment for a few of the samples in list ii at the beginning of this investigation. Those in list i will be demonstrated, and the observations for the remainder in list ii can be obtained from other members of the class.

Part f

Use the book of data to complete column F of the chart. Arrange the elements in order of increasing relative atomic mass. Do groups of similar elements occur together on this list?

Write the names of the first eight elements in a horizontal row. Underneath these write the names of the next eight elements, and so on. Note where potassium has been placed. Does this mean the breakdown of a possible pattern?

lithium	beryllium			neon
sodium				
potassium				
rubidium				

Using the information in columns A–E of your chart, how many patterns can you discover in this classification of elements? The usefulness of this classification will be illustrated in the following investigations.

Investigation 14.9 Predicting the properties of lithium

Some properties of sodium and potassium will be demonstrated by your teacher. Find the position of lithium in the periodic table.
►Predict the action (a) of heat, (b) of water and (c) of chlorine, on lithium. ◄

Investigation 14.10 Testing the prediction

You will need

beaker, 100 cm³
broken crucible, or lid, or asbestos paper
tongs
Bunsen burner and asbestos square
safety goggles
universal indicator solution
small piece of lithium
N.B. – Lithium is caustic and should not be allowed to touch the skin, clothes, etc.

Part a

Place a small piece of lithium no bigger than a rice grain on a crucible lid or piece of broken porcelain. Hold the crucible lid with tongs and warm it with a small flame. Does the lithium burn in the air? Notice the colour of the flame.

Allow the residue to cool and then put a few drops of water onto it. Does it dissolve? Test the water with universal indicator paper.

136

Part b

Pour water into a beaker until it is about half full, and put a small piece of lithium no larger than a rice grain on the water. Note what happens.

Part c

Test the water with universal indicator paper.

The action of chlorine on lithium will be demonstrated by your teacher. These metals are called alkali metals.

Investigation 14.11 Predicting the properties of iodine

Some properties of chlorine and bromine will be demonstrated by your teacher. Find the position of iodine in the periodic table. ►Predict the action (a) of water, (b) of sodium hydroxide solution and (c) of iron wool on iodine.◄

Investigation 14.12 Testing the prediction

You will need

two hard glass test tubes, 100 × 16 mm
Bunsen burner
small crystals of iodine
iron wool
sodium hydroxide solution
universal indicator paper

137

Part a

Test the solubility of iodine in cold water. Warm the water and test with universal indicator paper.

Part b

Repeat the experiment with sodium hydroxide solution. How do your observations compare with those made for chlorine and bromine?

Part c

Place a small crystal of iodine in the bottom of a hard glass test tube. Push a tuft of iron wool about half way down the tube and heat it thoroughly (if necessary, warm the iodine gently to vaporise it). Is there evidence that an interaction is taking place? Compare this reaction with the similar reactions with chlorine and bromine.

The Nuffield Chemistry background book *The periodic table* gives an historical survey of the classification pattern of the elements.

▷Investigation 14.13 Investigating some other metals

You will need

five hard glass test tubes, 100 × 16 mm
Bunsen burner
samples of oxides of:
copper
nickel
iron
cobalt
manganese
dilute hydrochloric acid
concentrated hydrochloric acid
copper foil
nickel foil
iron wire

Place a spatula measure of each of the oxides in a test tube and add half a test tube of dilute hydrochloric acid. Warm until the oxide has dissolved. In some cases it may be necessary to add a little concentrated hydrochloric acid (take care!) and to filter or centri-

138

fuge to get a clear solution. Note the colour of the resulting solution in each case.

Test the metal samples for strength and ductility. How do their physical properties compare with the alkali metals? Try the action of cold and warm water on the metals.

▷**Investigation 14.14 Elements in nature**

The periodic table below shows how metals occur in nature (the table is an elaboration of the one you used earlier).

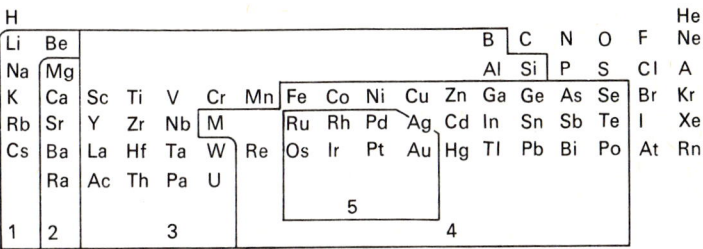

Figure 14.6

1 soluble salts extracted electrolytically.
2 mainly insoluble salts extracted electrolytically.
3 insoluble oxides, aluminosilicate and silicate rocks extracted by various processes.
4 often found as sulphides. Roasted to form oxides and then converted to metal.
5 native.

The following table shows the approximate concentrations at which various ores are worked. (ppm is an abbreviation for parts per million.)

product	level	product	level
diamonds	<1 ppm	copper	1–3%
gold	8 ppm	lead	2–12%
tin (alluvial)	0.01%	iron	30–68%
uranium	0.1%	fluorite	30–70%
nickel	1%	sulphur	20–98%

The prices quoted on 17 May 1972 for the various products which are listed are shown below:

diamonds (industrial) £1 per carat
gold $54.60 per fine oz
tin £1.473 per metric ton
uranium $5.8 per lb
nickel £1.150 per ton
copper £430 per metric ton
lead £121.75 per metric ton
iron £3 per ton
fluorite £37.75 per 1 000 kilogramme
sulphur £31.89 per 1 000 kilogramme

Use the information on occurrence, extraction and level of working to give an explanation of the prices. Are there other important factors? What about demand?

Investigation 14.15 Mineral identification

Part a

You will need

malachite ore specimen

Examine and describe the specimen. ▶Carry out experiments to determine its composition. ◀

▷Part b

You will need

one granite specimen
one sample of crushed material derived from the granite
one hand lens
one mounted needle

Using the mounted needle separate the crushed material into piles of like particles. How many different materials can you find? Are the different particles present in approximately equal proportions?

Read the second half of the book *Rocks and minerals*. Then make a table in your note-book as follows:

lustre	colour	hardness	cleavage	identification
non-metallic, glassy	light, grey to colourless	six or over	absent conchoidal fracture	quartz (SiO_2)

Using keys 5, 6, 7 and 8 in *Rocks and minerals*, fill in the details of your observations and identifications for each of the different materials you have found in the crushed sample. If time permits, you could try this with other granite specimens.

▷**Investigation 14.16 Classifying planets**

The following table gives 'large-scale' information about the planets in the solar system. Until recent years little else was known about them.

name of planet	approximate mass/10^{24} kg	approximate diameter/ 10^6 m	approximate density/ 10^3 kg m^{-3}	average distance from Sun/ 10^{11} m	number of satellites	orbital period/ years
Mercury	0.3	5	5.4	0.6	0	0.24
Venus	5.4	13	5.0	1.1	0	0.6
Earth	6.0	13	5.5	1.5	1	1.0
Mars	0.7	6	3.9	2.3	2	1.9
Jupiter	1 900	150	1.3	7.8	12	11.9
Saturn	570	125	0.7	14.3	9	29.5
Uranus	90	50	1.6	28.8	5	84
Neptune	100	50	2.3	45	2	165
Pluto	1★	6★	5★	59	0	250
Sun	2×10^6	1 400	1.4	–	–	–

★These figures are uncertain

Part a

Classify the planets into what you consider the best number of subsets on the basis of:
  i mass only
 ii diameter only
iii density only
iv distance from the Sun only

141

Figure 14.7
Photograph of Saturn

v number of satellites only
vi orbital period only.
      Is any one of these classifications obviously the best? Does any one present particular problems?

Part b

Use all of the criteria above to classify the planets into a suitable number of subsets. (You do not need to give equal weighting to each.) Do you regard this as more satisfactory than any of the classifications in part a? Give your reasons.

Part c

Discuss the usefulness of your classification in any attempt to explain the origin of the solar system. Would it be improved by including any of the following information? If so which, and what difference would it make?

i The plane of the orbit of every planet except Mercury and Pluto is within 4° of the plane of the Earth's orbit.

ii The angle between the Equator and the plane of the orbit is between 23° and 29° for most planets. The exceptions are Jupiter (3°) and Uranus (about 100°). The angles are not known for Mercury and Pluto.

Part d

There is a mathematical pattern concerning the distances of the planets from the Sun, which was proposed in 1766 by Titius (a

142

German astronomer) and publicised by Bode (who was also a German) in 1772. Consequently it is called the Titius-Bode law.

The pattern is best understood as an arithmetical sequence:

$$\frac{4+0}{10}, \quad \frac{4+3}{10}, \quad \frac{4+6}{10}, \quad \frac{4+12}{10}, \quad \frac{4+24}{10}, \quad \frac{4+48}{10}, \quad \ldots$$

How is each term formed from the previous one? What is the next term?

The table below gives the values of these compared with the distances of the planets from the Sun expressed in astronomical units (a.u.), which is the distance from the Sun to the Earth.

planet	distance from Sun/a.u.	Titius-Bode value
Mercury	0.38	0.4
Venus	0.72	0.7
Earth	1.00	1.0
Mars	1.52	1.6
–	–	2.8
Jupiter	5.2	5.2
Saturn	9.5	10.0
Uranus	19.2	19.6
Neptune	30.1	–
Pluto	39.4	38.8

Discuss the significance and the usefulness of this rule. ▶Use it to predict where another planet might be found. Is there any limit to the number of planets the rule will predict? ◀

▷15 Distribution of building blocks

In this (entirely optional) section you will be answering the question: 'Is building block distribution a result of interaction?'. There will be a general look at building blocks first in your locality, then in your country, in the world and finally in our solar system. A more detailed look at the distribution of a building block of your choice will complete the section. This is in the form of an optional long term project.

▷**Investigation 15.1 Building blocks in the locality**

Carry out a general survey of your locality:
a Comment on the variety and types of living building blocks in your area.
b What is the nature of, and the differences between, the major ionic, molecular or giant structure building blocks?
c Are the major living and non-living building blocks evenly or unevenly distributed?

   Discussion in class will indicate how to look for answers to these questions.

Figure 15.1
The distribution of two organism building blocks: the Adonis Blue butterfly (right) and the horse-shoe vetch (far right). The horse-shoe vetch is virtually the only food plant of the caterpillars of the Adonis Blue whose distribution reflects this interaction. Use a geological map to discover if the distribution of the vetch itself is possibly determined by any other building blocks

144

Can you offer any explanation for the distributions? Does the presence (or absence) of any particular building block have any effect on the presence (or absence) of other building blocks.

These are complex questions which you will be unable to answer in detail. Figure 15.1 illustrates how the presence of one building block influences the distribution of another.

▷**Investigation 15.2 Building blocks in my country**

You will need

reference books

Use an atlas to discover how building blocks like iron, coal, water and grassland are distributed in your country. Is there an even distribution? Does the distribution have any effect on the distribution of other building blocks?

What happens to the people in an area when, for example, a coal mine is shut? Should we be concerned about these effects? What can be done both by and for the people concerned?

▷**Investigation 15.3 Building blocks throughout the world**

You will need

reference books

Figure 15.2
World distribution of the tapir

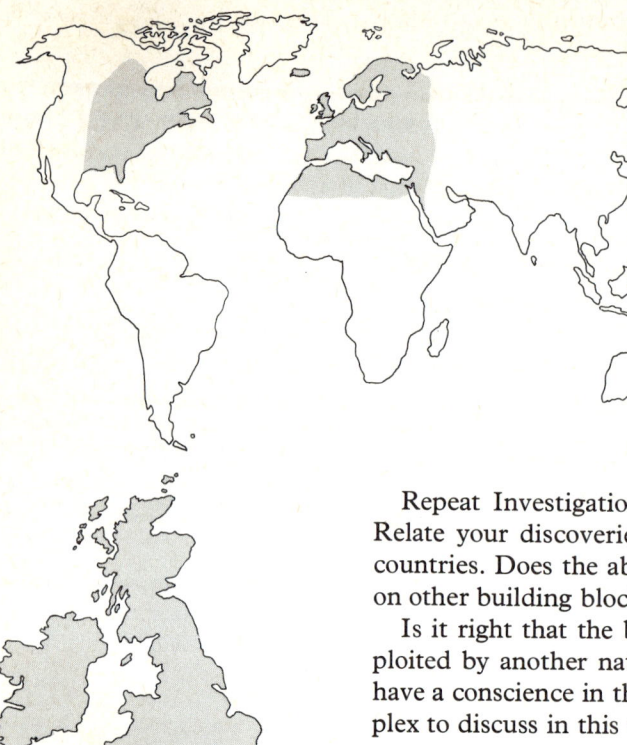

Figure 15.3
The World and British Isles
distribution of the red-admiral
butterfly (*Vanessa atalanta*)

Repeat Investigation 15.2, but this time for the whole world. Relate your discoveries to the standards of living in the various countries. Does the absence of one building block have any effect on other building blocks?

Is it right that the building blocks of one nation should be exploited by another nation which has plenty? Do nations seem to have a conscience in this respect? Or are these questions too complex to discuss in this way?

Figure 15.4
Which countries mine coal? Why are diamonds so valuable?

▷ Investigation 15.4 The planet building block

You could refer to the Longman Physics Topics book *Planetary astronomy*. Is there an even distribution of planets in our solar system? Use reference books to read about the regularity of motion of the different planets. How does this regularity affect us? With what do the planets seem to interact?

What pattern of distribution of building blocks emerges from the previous investigations? ▶ You should now take a closer look at one of the building blocks in an attempt to discover why it is distributed in a particular way. You could present your findings as a wall chart, as a project book, or as a lecture. ◀

Note – These are just suggestions: you might wish to choose a different building block. All are fairly long-term studies and should not be attempted unless worthwhile projects will result. The questions are not exhaustive; you might think of other areas of study.

▷ Investigation 15.5 A closer look at building block distribution

▶ The whole of this investigation is in the form of a problem.

Part a   Structural materials

What building stones are used in your district? What are their sources? Are they easily weathered?

Collect samples of local building stone; perform experiments and use reference books to answer the following questions: Are the materials cheap or expensive? What colour are they? Do they break easily? Are they porous? Are they associated with high or low land? Do they supply any raw materials to the chemical industry? (You might like to draw a flow diagram.) Link your answers to the way(s) in which the building block is distributed.

Part b   Man (and society)

Carry out surveys to answer these questions. In which country were people in your area born? What are living conditions like in your district? What are they like in nearby districts? What is the average family size in your district? What is the density of housing and people? What are the main places of employment for people in your locality? Does place of employment have any effect on the way these people are distributed? Do people having certain jobs

147

live in particular districts? What building blocks have an effect on where people live? 'The Park Hill story' from the *Patterns* book *Science and decision-making* would make interesting reading here.

Part c   Why are organisms unevenly distributed?

Choose an organism building block. Devise a method to measure its distribution quantitatively. Attempt to answer the question posed in the problem.

Compare the distribution of the species of *Papaver* as shown in figures 15.5–8. These plants are annuals and reproduce only once in their lives. The average number of seeds formed by a single plant of each species has been calculated as follows:

P. rhoeas	170 000
P. dubium	13 700
P. argemone	2 142
P. hybridum	1 680

Figure 15.5
Distribution of the long prickly-headed poppy
(*P. argemone*)

Figure 15.6
Distribution of field poppy
(*P. rhoeas*)

Figure 15.7
Distribution of rough poppy
(*P. hybridum*)

Figure 15.8
Distribution of the long
headed poppy
(*P. dubium*)

How would you account for the distribution shown in the maps above (figures 15.5–8)?

Part d   Water

You might like to consider some of these questions: Is any of the water in your locality obtained from underground sources? Is the water 'hard' or 'soft'? How could it be softened?

Try some of the experiments.

How is the water purified? If your water comes from reservoirs, what is the shape of the dam? Why is it this shape?

Perform experiments to discover what types of solids and what types of liquids are (a) soluble and (b) insoluble in water? What is the water used for? (The diagram shown in figure 15.9 on next page might be of interest and help.) ◀

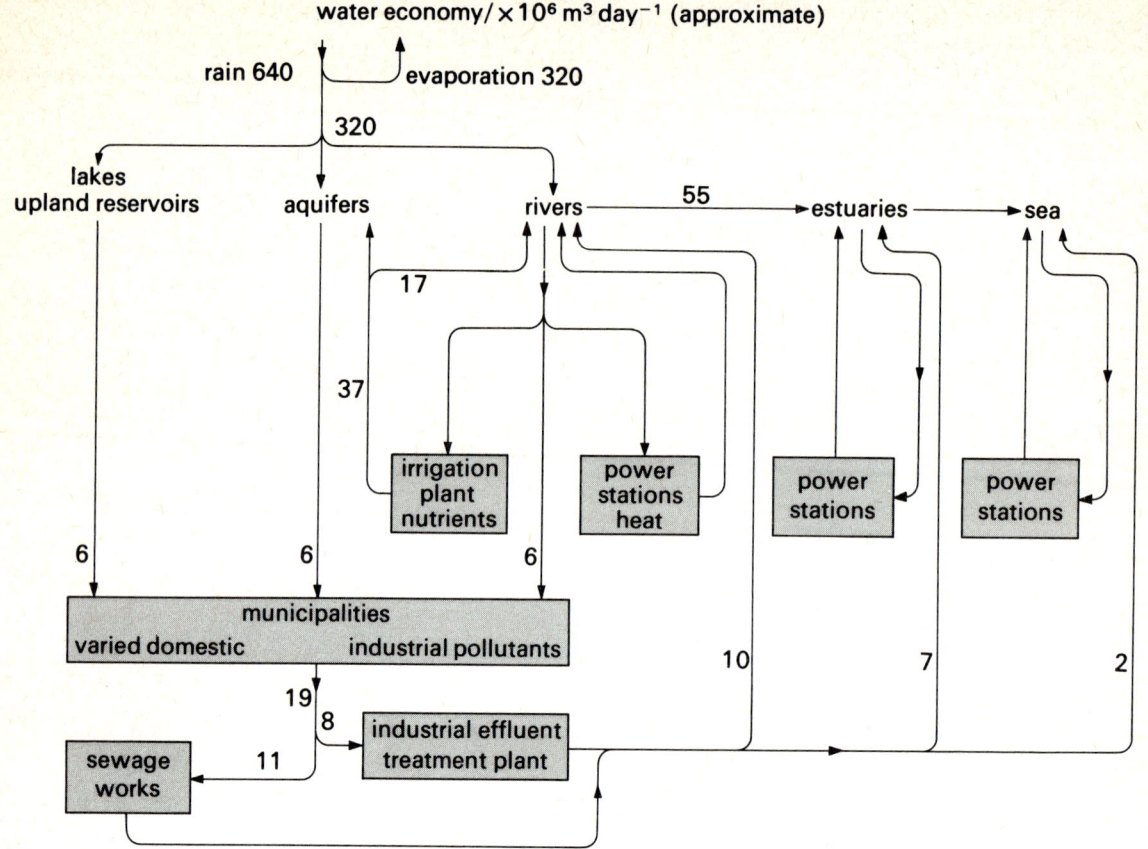

water economy/ × 10⁶ m³ day⁻¹ (approximate)

Figure 15.9

Appendix
Vectors and displacements

This appendix is for those who have not covered the mathematics which is necessary for Section 13, 'Motion'.

Investigation A.1   Journeys

A map is always useful on a journey, so let us consider one first (figure A.1).

Part a

You may already know how to give a map reference. If not, read carefully the explanation beside the map. You can ignore the letters in the Full Reference, and use only the figures. What is indicated at the following points?
a 841151
b 831188
c 898160
d 853185.
 Find the map reference for:
a a school
b a church with a spire
c a road-over-rail bridge
d a hill steeper than 1 in 7.

Part b

In some ways a map reference is similar to the coordinates of a point on a graph. Make a list of the similarities. Make another list of the differences. How many numbers (not figures) make up a map reference? How many figures make up each number? When would fewer figures be adequate? In future the numbers will be separated by a comma: (810, 104).

Part c

Suppose you started from the church at Haresfield (810, 104) and travelled to the milestone at Green Street (888, 152). There are

TO GIVE A GRID REFERENCE CORRECT TO 100 METRES

EXAMPLE		Churcham Ho	
See diagram on left for Grid Letters. They are SO			
East		**North**	
Take west edge of kilometre square in which point lies and read the large figures printed opposite this line on north or south margins.	75	Take south edge of kilometre square in which point lies and read the large figures printed opposite this line on east or west margins.	19
	1		3
Estimate tenths Eastwards	751	*Estimate tenths Northwards*	193
Full 100 Metre Reference SO 751193			

The above Full Reference is unique. For many purposes the first grid letter can be omitted, giving a reference, O 751193 which recurs at intervals of 500 Kilometres. If both grid letters are omitted, the resulting reference 751193 recurs at intervals of 100 Kilometres. When the area concerned is sufficiently restricted, as will usually be the case with maps on scales of one inch to the mile and larger, both the grid letters are normally omitted

Roads

Ministry of Transport
- Motorway — M 5 or A 1 (M)
- Trunk — A 38 (T)
- Class 1 — Single & Dual Carriageway — A 4103
- ,, 2 — B 4215

14 ft of Metalling or over (not included above)

Under 14 ft of Metalling
- Tarred (not included above)
- Untarred ,,

TOLL
Gate

Minor Road in towns, Drive or Track (unmetalled)
(unfenced roads are shown by pecked lines)

Under Construction

Steep Gradient 1 in 5 or steeper ◄ 1 in 7 to under 1 in 5 ◄

Path

Heights in feet above Mean Sea Level
- surveyed by levelling · 275
- not surveyed by levelling · 1091

Triangulation Pillar △

Intersection, Lat & Long at 5' intervals +
(not shown where it confuses important detail)

Church or Chapel
- with Tower
- with Spire
- without Tower or Spire

Wireless or TV Mast 人   Wind Pump

Windmill (in use)   (disused)

Lighthouse   Lightship

Town Hall, Guildhall or equivalent   TH

Public House   PH   Post Office   P

Club House   CH

Mile Stone   .MS   Telephone Call Box

Mile Post   .MP

Public Convenience (in rural areas)   .PC

Roman Antiquity (AD43 to AD420)   VILLA

Other Antiquities   Castle

Site of Antiquity   +

Site of Battle (with date)   1066

{ PO .T
  AA .A
  RAC .R

Public Paths
- Footpath (right of way on foot)
- Bridleway (right of way on foot and on horseback)

Road used as public path

Part of
SHEET 143

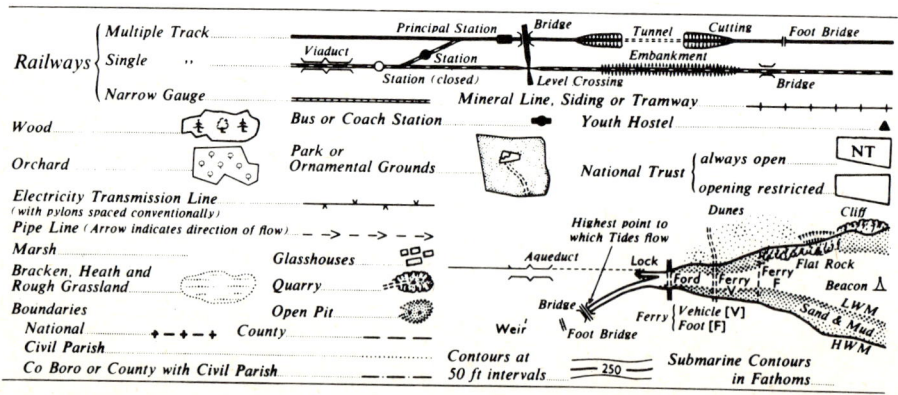

Railways
- Multiple Track
- Single ,,
- Narrow Gauge

Principal Station   Bridge   Tunnel   Cutting   Foot Bridge
Viaduct   Station   Embankment
Station (closed)   Level Crossing   Bridge
Mineral Line, Siding or Tramway

Wood

Orchard

Bus or Coach Station   Youth Hostel

Park or Ornamental Grounds   National Trust
- always open — NT
- opening restricted

Electricity Transmission Line
(with pylons spaced conventionally)

Pipe Line (Arrow indicates direction of flow)

Highest point to which Tides flow

Dunes   Cliff

Aqueduct   Lock

Marsh

Glasshouses

Flat Rock
Beacon

Bracken, Heath and Rough Grassland   Quarry

Boundaries   Open Pit

Bridge   Ford   Ferry   Sand & Mud   LWM

Weir   Foot Bridge   Ferry   Vehicle [V]   Foot [F]   HWM

National   County

Civil Parish

Co Boro or County with Civil Parish   Contours at 50 ft intervals — 250 —   Submarine Contours in Fathoms

Public paths and roads used as public paths have been derived from Definitive Maps available on 1st February 1968 (as amended in part by enactments or instruments)
The representation of any other roads, tracks or paths is no evidence of the existence of a right of way

Figure A.1

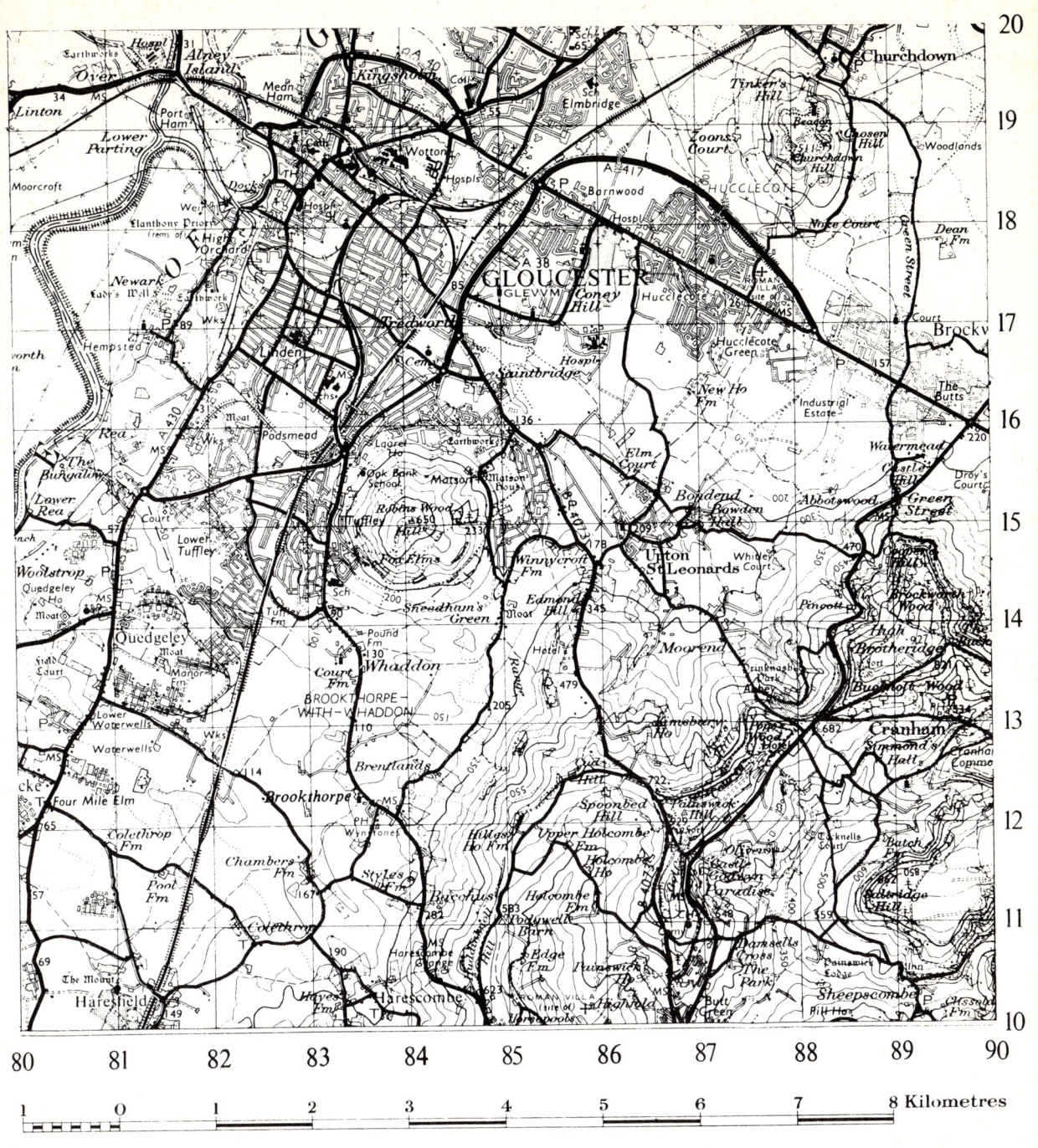

Scale:

several ways to make the journey, but in the end you would be the same distance east and north of your starting point, whichever route you took. How far east of your starting point would you be? How far north of your starting point?

Now imagine a journey from Four Mile Elm (803, 123) to someone's house at (881, 171). How far east do you go? How far north? What can you say about this journey compared with the previous one?

What about a journey, from Quedgeley House (802, 143) to the beacon at (883, 191)?

Find another journey which is equivalent to these three. What has to be the same? What can be different?

These journeys are often called displacements. Every displacement has at least two parts or components (some displacements need more than two). On a map displacement, the distance east (the easting) is always given before the distance north (the northing).

What would be your finishing point if you started from Haresfield Church (810, 104) but went 4.8 km north and 7.8 km east instead of 4.8 km east and 7.8 km north?

Does the order of the numbers make any difference to the displacement?

Part d

There is a very useful way of representing displacements (or journeys) using vectors. (If you have done a modern mathematics course you will possibly have met the idea already.) In mathematics a vector means a set of numbers in a certain order. You are working with the simplest sort of vector, with only two numbers.

The journey 4.8 km east and 7.8 km north is usually represented by the vector $\begin{pmatrix} 48 \\ 78 \end{pmatrix}$. What vectors would represent these journeys?

a From Chambers' Farm (829, 116) to Kimsbury House (865, 130),
b from Oak Bank School (836, 155) to Matson's House (848, 155),
c from the Bus Station (835, 187) to the A46/A417 roundabout (898, 160),
d from Kimsbury House (865, 130) to Chambers' Farm (829, 116).

Part e

By now you have probably realised that a map reference itself is a vector. Suggest a reason why two different sorts of vector are used for a map reference and for a displacement.

$\begin{pmatrix} 48 \\ 78 \end{pmatrix}$ is called a column-vector,

(865, 130) is called a row-vector.

Some books write both displacement vectors and position vectors as row-vectors. Why could this be confusing?

Part f

Suppose you made a journey (displacement) represented by the vector $\begin{pmatrix} 16 \\ 11 \end{pmatrix}$ and then another journey (displacement) represented by the vector $\begin{pmatrix} 5 \\ 6 \end{pmatrix}$. What vector would represent your total displace-

ment? If you do not see the answer at once, write down in words what the separate displacements are. What is the rule (or pattern) for combining the vectors representing displacements?

This rule applies to any sort of vector. Later in the course you will meet vectors representing several other sorts of quantity besides displacements. What is the pattern (or rule) which must be obeyed if a quantity can be represented by a vector?

Use the rule for combining vectors to find the total displacement in these cases:

a 4.5 km and 2.1 km north, followed by 1.2 km east and 1.2 km north,

b 1.5 km east and 1.7 km north, followed by 1.2 km west and 0.1 km north,

c 1.5 km east and 1.7 km north, followed by 2.1 km west and 1.5 km south.

Use the same rule to find out in the following cases what displacement is needed to complete the journey.

d Total displacement, 6.2 km east, 4.5 km north. Displacement so far, 4.2 km east, 1.5 km north.

e Total displacement, 3.9 km east, 6.0 km north. Displacement so far, 1.2 km east, 5.2 km north.

f Total displacement, 3.5 km east, 1.5 km north. Displacement so far, 3.5 km east, 0.4 km north.

g Total displacement, 4.2 km east, 2.4 km north. Displacement so far, 5.6 km east, 1.8 km north.

h Total displacement, 1.8 km east, 1.5 km north. Displacement so far, 2.9 km east, 2.0 km north.

Part g

▷We are used to using east and north as 'standard' directions. Would it make any difference to the actual journey (displacement) from, for example, Chambers' Farm to Kimsbury House, if some-one worked out components based on different standard directions, for example N 30° E and N 60° W? What would be different? Figure A.2 should help you.

Figure A.2

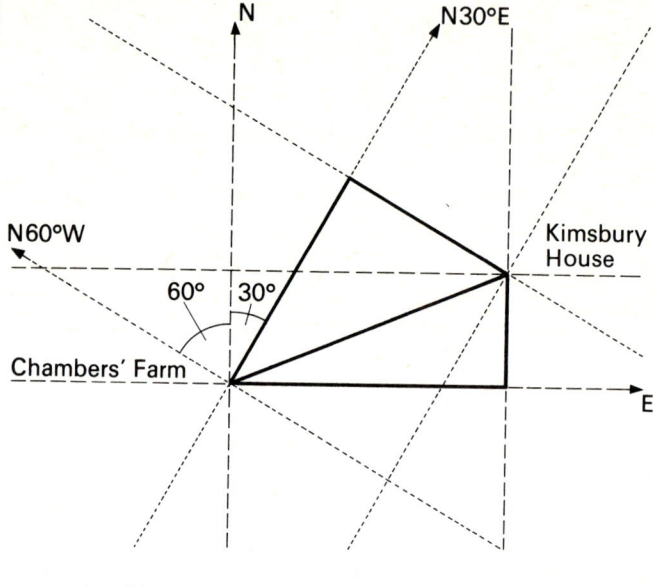

‐ ‐ ‐ ‐ Lines running east and north
⋯⋯⋯⋯ Lines running N60°W and N30°E

Part h

▷ In a fairly small area such as the British Isles a map reference based on a flat map is perfectly adequate. Why is this system un-suitable for use on a world-wide scale? What system is used for referring to points anywhere on the Earth's surface? Can vectors be used to represent displacements in this system?

Part i

▷ What system is used to refer to the apparent position of stars in the sky? Find out the meaning of 'declination' and 'right ascension'. Can vectors be used to represent displacements in this system? Why is it only the apparent position which can be specified using two numbers? Why is this not a very great restriction in practice for astronomers?

Investigation A.2 Distance and displacement

1 There is a road bridge over a stream near Colethrop at (828, 108).

156

What is the displacement from here to the road junction at B 4073 at (858, 148)? What is the straight-line distance between these two points (as the crow flies)?

To find the answer to the last question you had to use a mathematical pattern about right-angled triangles. What is this pattern? Express it using x and y for the east and north components respectively, and r for the total distance.

2 Estimate the total distance you travel during a typical school day from the moment you get out of bed in the morning to the moment you go to bed at night. What is your total displacement?

3 Make a plan of your school, and use it to work out your displacements in changing rooms during the course of the day.

4 You cycle round your school from F to G in a semi-circle of radius 50 m as shown in figure A.3. What is the distance you cycle? What is your final displacement from your starting point? You then cycle back again. What total distance have you cycled? What is your total displacement?

Figure A.3

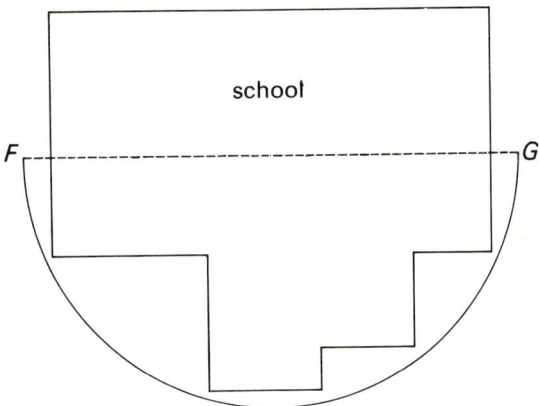

5 A test driver drives a new model round a track of total length 6 km at a steady speed of $40\,\mathrm{m\,s^{-1}}$. After 50 full laps what is the displacement of the car from its starting point? What is the distance it has travelled?

6 What is the displacement of the Earth after six months? What is its displacement after twelve months? (Distance from the Earth to the Sun $= 1.5 \times 10^{10}$ m.) In giving these answers, what assumptions do you make about an 'origin' and about specifying directions?

7 Starting from one of the central squares on a chess board what displacements are allowed for a rook, a bishop, a queen and a knight?

8 What is the displacement of Accra from London using latitude and longitude? Of Bogota from Accra? Of New York from Bogota? Of New York from London? Could you calculate the distance of New York from London using Pythagoras' theorem? Explain your answer.

Investigation A.3 Combining other sorts of displacement

1 If you draw a line down the page 50 mm long and your partner then moves the book 30 mm to the left while you keep the pencil still, what is the displacement of the pencil point from its starting point, relative to the book? If you drew the line and your partner moved the book both at the same time, what difference would this make to the displacement? How would your answers be affected if the two movements were not at right angles? What can you say in general about the result of adding two displacements:

a one after the other
b both at the same time?

2 Suppose that a man moves as shown in figure A.4 across the deck of a ship. While he does so the ship moves forward through the water. How could you find his total (resultant) displacement relative to the water? Is it necessary to use any particular set of axes and components? Is it necessary to use components at all?

3 Suppose the ship was in a current, and while the man was moving the water was displaced as shown in figure A.5. How would you find the displacement of the man relative to the water? Explain the fact that the answer would be the same whether you:

Figure A.4

p displacement of man relative to ship
q displacement of ship relative to water

Figure A.5

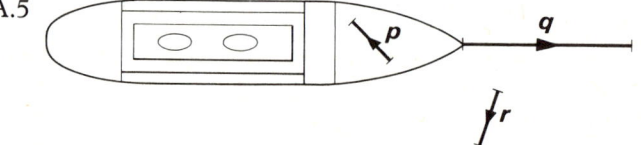

p displacement of man relative to ship
q displacement of ship relative to water
r displacement of water relative to land

Figure A.6

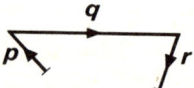

p displacement of man relative to ship
q displacement of ship relative to water
r displacement of water relative to land

158

a put the arrows representing the displacements end to end in order as shown in figure A.6
b found components in directions along and across the ship and added these (taking account of negatives)
c found components in directions east and north and added these (taking account of negatives).

Investigation A.4 Three-dimensional displacements

a The photograph (figure A.7) shows a school with one single-storey block and two blocks with several storeys. A new ceiling light has to be fixed in one of the rooms in the single-storey block. How many numbers would be needed to specify to the electrician where the light is needed? Why would the same answer not be sufficient for the other blocks? How many numbers would be needed in this case?

b Taking the main door of the building you are in as origin, and choosing suitable axes, estimate the coordinates of the door into the room you are in (working in metres). It is usual to give co-ordinates in the order of axes x, y, z (in other words 'to the right,

Figures A.7

forwards, upwards'). Express the coordinates as a row-vector. Choose another room, for preference on a different floor but in the same building. Estimate the coordinates of its door, and express these as another row-vector.

Now work out the displacement from the door of your room to the door of the other room and express this as a column-vector. What is the maximum number of components that could be required to do this in any building? Why do we refer to solid objects as '3D'?

c When you are considering displacements using maps, you are concerned with only two components, the eastings and the northings. But in fact a third component is needed to specify a point completely. What is the third component? How is it represented on the map? In what units is it represented?

d The journeys in Investigation A.1 can now be specified more completely. Here they are again, but with the (estimated) heights inserted. Give the column 3-vector representation in each case of the displacement. The heights are in feet.

i Chambers' Farm (829, 116, 150) to Kimsbury House (865, 130, 550)
ii Oak Bank School (838, 155, 200) to Matson's House (848, 155, 200)
iii Bus Station (835, 187, 50) to A46/A417 roundabout (898, 160, 220)
iv Kimsbury House (865, 130, 550) to Chambers' Farm (829, 116, 150).

e ▷ In Investigation A.2a you used Pythagoras' theorem to find the straight-line distance between the bridge near Colethrop at (828, 108) and the road junction at (858, 148). The height of each point is the same (about 160 feet above sea level), so the distance worked out correctly when you ignored heights.

Suggest a way to work out the distance in a straight line between two points not at the same height, as in example (a) above. Do not forget that the first two components are in 100 m units, but the third component is in feet. Figure A.8 will help you. 400 feet ≈ 122m.

Figure A.8

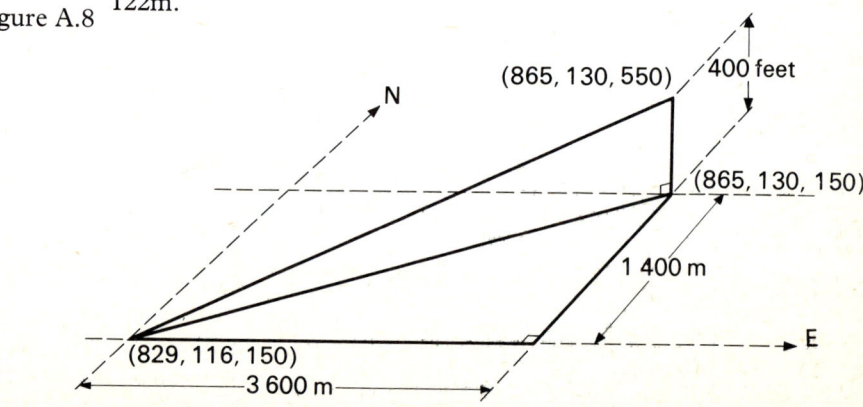

Index

Bold figures indicate illustrations.